the sweet
Gospel

To the One who is worthy,
from whom and to whom are all things,
both in Heaven and in earth, forever and ever.
Thank you for saving me, Jesus.
Father God, I'm so glad you can use the weakest of things,
because my efforts here fall short in every way.
Holy Spirit, I pray that you would do whatever you will
with all of my life and all of my words.
You are everything, and I am nothing.

the sweet Gospel

13 Weeks of Savoring the Good News

Mandy Ballard

Prescott
Publishing

Printed in cooperation with Prescott Publishing
3668 Southwood Dr.
Tyler, TX 75707

Scripture quotations are from the ESV® Bible (The Holy Bible, English Standard Version®), copyright ©2001 by Crossway, a publishing ministry of Good News Publishers. Used by permission. All rights reserved.

Cover art by Ira Khroniuk.

ISBN: 978-1-938945-28-1
LCCN: 2016952293

Contents

Foreword: A Heart for Jesus — vi

What is the Gospel? — 1

Why Study It? — 7

The Purpose of this Bible Study — 9

Week 1 – The Bible: Who, What, When, Where, How — 11

Week 2 – God: Loving and Eternal Creator — 19

Week 3 – Man, Sin, and the Fall — 29

Week 4 – Jesus: God in the Flesh — 39

Week 5 – The Perfect Sacrifice: Why We Needed It — 49

Week 6 – The Gift of Salvation and Repentance — 59

Week 7 – Leaving Behind the Darkness — 69

Week 8 – Believing and Following Jesus Now — 77

Week 9 – The Holy Spirit: Our Gift — 85

Week 10 – Grace Upon Grace: When We Stumble — 95

Week 11 – The Transforming Power of the Gospel — 105

Week 12 – Seeking God's Will in Our Lives — 115

Week 13 – Walking in Joy with an Eternity Mindset — 125

Conclusion — 137

Acknowledgements — 139

About the Author — 141

Foreword

A Heart for Jesus

Several months ago, my family had the privilege of spending an evening and sharing a meal in the home of Robert and Mandy Ballard. Families with as many children as we have don't get treated to dinner very often, and it is a testimony to the Ballards' lavish generosity and gracious hospitality that they braved such an invitation in the first place. The food they served us was wholesome and delicious, but more satisfying still was the conversation around the dinner table.

On the way home afterward, my husband and I were discussing with our children the evening we'd just enjoyed when I posed the question, "Do you know what I love most about the Ballards?"

Every child immediately piped up with an animated guess:

"They're good cooks!"

"They have a beautiful home!"

"They're nice to one another!"

"They're nice to *us*!"

"They're smart!"

"Their children are well behaved!"

"They have red hair!"

The answers kept flying until, laughing, I shushed the kids so I could finish my statement. "All those things are true," I told them, "but none of that is what I had in mind. The thing I love most about the Ballards is that they have such a heart for Jesus. And they're constantly on the lookout for ways to share Christ's love with others more effectively."

It was Mandy's deep love for Jesus and her gratitude for all He has done for us that compelled her to write a series of blog posts called "Walking through the Gospel." Having recently read several of the posts in that series, I asked her about them over dinner. If you ever want to see Rob and Mandy Ballard's eyes light up with sincere, excited, uncontainable joy, just steer the conversation to Christ's finished work on the cross—if they don't beat you to it! Their enthusiasm for the sweet gospel message is both palpable and contagious.

And so it was during that delightful dinner that we first began to discuss the possibility of turning Mandy's blog series into the book you now hold in your hands. The project took a little longer to complete than either of us anticipated, but I'm so thankful Mandy agreed to let me help with the formatting and publishing.

Psalm 34:8 tells us, *"Taste and see that the LORD is good; blessed is the one who takes refuge in Him."* It is the sincere prayer of both our families that if you have never savored the sweet gospel of Jesus Christ, the pages of this book will inspire you to do so without delay.

Blessings,

Jennifer Flanders
author of *Balance: The Art of Minding What Matters Most*

What is the Gospel?

Gala apples are *delectable*.

They are tangy, a bit earthy even; soft, yet crisp. Moist and delicate, the sweetness of those apples lingers on your tongue after each bite. Nothing else tastes quite like them. They are *incredibly* delicious.

Can you imagine tasting a fresh Gala apple right now?

You can only accurately understand the taste of the fruit I'm describing if you've experienced it before.

Imagine if I told you about the apple, but you had never had one before. Imagine you had never tasted something tangy or something sweet. I could describe the apple to you in hundreds of different ways, but you won't truly be able to understand what I'm talking about until you take that first bite.

Experience allows us to understand descriptions. We frame the meanings of the words others use by what we ourselves have experienced in real life. Your tongue has to have tasted "tangy" in order for me to be able to fully communicate what the word means. Once you've experienced "tangy," you *know* what it means.

Much like the apples, you have to experience the Gospel before you can fully understand it. My words alone can't give you the true experience of the Gospel.

We can define it, we can explain it in detail—but do our *hearts* truly understand what the Gospel means?

We can talk about it for days, but the power of the Gospel doesn't truly come through words alone. *Explaining will never give you the experience.* The true understanding of the Gospel is found in the very depths of our soul and can only be understood once you've experienced its power.

The truth of the Gospel is this: God the Father, in His infinite wisdom, created the world, sent His Son to die for the very people who sinned against Him. His mercy redeemed those whom He chose for the purpose of bringing glory and honor and praise to His name.

We exist for the glory of God. Not for our own sake, but for the name of God to be made great. God is the center of our world—of our lives—because He is *God.*

In our sinful rebellion, we left God behind and sought after ourselves and our own pleasures. Every single one of us. *"All of us have sinned and fall short of the glory of God."* (Romans 3:23)

Standing in horrific pride against the Creator of the entire universe, we desired to make our *own name* great. We desired to serve ourselves in this time on the earth.

We rebelled against God, and we deserve to be separated from Him. For eternity. Who can stand before the very God of all and demand that we deserve anything in light of what we've done? When that final day comes, could you possibly stand and say, "God, why are you so unjust to send me away to be separated from You for eternity?"

Would you dare to demand that you deserve a second chance? We cannot even stand on our feet without God willing it to happen. Who could say anything in response to Him? Oh, we are so full of sin and pride.

But God still loved us!

Why? Not because of any redeeming quality we had. He loved us because *He is loving.* He created us, He wrote the plan of salvation before the foundation of the world, for His glory. Not for anything else.

If you feel a welling up of resistance in your chest to that statement, you are feeling the very thing we all need to be redeemed from: pride.

God *is* GLORY. God is HOLY. God is JUST. He is the Alpha and the

Omega. The beginning and the end. And we are nothing but dust. We have nothing in light of Him. Yet in the most incredible way, He lowered Himself to our status and came in human form to live as we do, so that we could be rescued from the very sin that condemned us to eternal separation from God.

Jesus came and fulfilled the laws of God and sacrificed Himself—a spotless Lamb. He defeated the power of sin and death through His resurrection, so that we could be made new. So that we could be made righteous, like Him. So that we could become His sons and daughters.

Do you see it? Do you understand?

You are desperately in need of Jesus. You have nothing to offer God. He is EVERYTHING. God doesn't need you to do anything for Him. *You need Him.*

The Holy Father has provided a way for you to fellowship with Him again. You could never be good enough or moral enough to get there on your own. No amount of singing His praise, no amount of being good to others, no amount of following of the Bible, no amount of offering thanksgiving will ever bring you to salvation. You cannot offer God anything in exchange for His grace. Matt Chandler says it so well in *The Explicit Gospel*:

> If everything is God's, you have nothing to give him that he doesn't already own. This means that you cannot put him into your debt. And this means, alternately, that God owes no man anything. Our very existence has been gifted to us by his grace.

You have nothing in comparison to His glory, and yet He offers you everything. Can you lose your pride, and admit that you are vile and desperate and in need of a Savior? That's what you have to do to truly understand the Gospel. You have been given a chance to be a child *of the one true and living God.*

Jesus gave up Himself, so that you could be a chosen one.

Friend, if you understand this, you cannot help but worship Him. He is Glory, the one unchangeable, unshakeable, undeniable God.

Do not reject Him! You have one chance in this life you've been given. You have one life to live. You've been given the gift of redemption. You have been given a chance to be saved from the consequences of your pride and sin. A chance you don't deserve in any way, shape, or form.

Will you accept the gift of salvation? Will you give your life to Christ?

The Gospel is the Good News. The news that God has redeemed you if you have faith in Him.

> ...*because, if you confess with your mouth that Jesus is Lord and believe in your heart that God raised him from the dead, you will be saved.* (Romans 10:9)

Confess that the Lord is God, and you are not. Confess that you are broken and desperate and in need of a Savior. Tell Him. Tell others. Believe that He has risen from the dead and conquered death so that you might understand His power.

Nothing on this earth is more important than this. No one—nothing—but Jesus can redeem you. He did it. For you. Because He loves you.

You are a creature made to glorify the God who redeemed you. You can choose to glorify and serve God in this time on the earth or you can choose to glorify and serve yourself. But I have to warn you, if you choose yourself, you will not spend eternity with God. You *can't.* You must have faith here and believe in Him on earth to receive the gift of salvation. One moment after death is too late. There are no do-overs.

Whom will you serve here? No serving two masters. It's you or Him. Will you choose to be His? And will you do it with all of you? Every single part of your life? That is what He requires, sweet friends. Give it all back to Him.

Nothing held back.

That is the power of the Gospel—the story of a merciful God giving life to the already dead! A heart that once was as hard as stone—a heart that served itself—becomes transformed into a new creation. A heart of stone becomes a heart of flesh when it is filled with the power of the Spirit of God. (Ezekiel 36:26) He has done it in me, and I can tell you that it's unlike anything I've experienced on this side of Heaven.

There is no one—no author, no song, no experience in nature—nothing

4

that speaks into my soul like His Spirit does. I can't describe how *powerful* His presence and love is in my heart. There is no one—not one single thing on this earth that arouses my heart to worship like His Spirit. He is worthy. Oh, how He is worthy.

Holy, holy, holy, is the Lord God Almighty! He is great in power and in might, and there is no God in Heaven or earth besides Him.

Will you serve Him with your life? Choose today. Live for Him today. Nothing else matters.

Why Study It?

"If you would follow on to know the Lord, come at once to the open Bible,
expecting it to speak to you. Do not come with the notion
that it is a thing which you may push around at your convenience.
It is more than a thing; it is a voice, a word, the very Word of the Living God."

-A.W. Tozer, *The Pursuit of God*

Many people long for a true relationship with God, and they are searching but have no idea where to start.

The best and only place to begin is in His Word, the Bible. We can't believe in Jesus based on what people say, or on what our friends tell us, without searching out the living Word of God.

His Word is truth. It's alive today—and we get to read it! Isn't that wonderful?

Falling in love with Jesus is entirely possible when we get to know Him! But it's so important that we take the time to study and understand Him—and that only happens when we read the Bible.

This is a human example, but imagine if you were dating someone. Suppose you had declared your love and were even making plans to marry this person, yet you had no desire to spend meaningful time together or get to know your "Beloved" better. You claim to "love" him, but you don't take time to get to know him? To hear about what he's done in the past, what he's working on in the present, what he hopes for the future?

How would such a relationship really ever work?

It wouldn't, right?

It's the same with God—falling in love with Him requires that we know Him on a deeper level than just by name. We need to spend time with Him every day, studying His Word and learning all we can about Him. The Lord gives us faith and love for Him—it's nothing we can do on our own, but getting to know who He is through His Word opens our eyes.

That's the goal of this book. I'm so excited—for the next 13 weeks, we're going to walk through the Gospel together! We're going to talk about who God is, who man is, where man stands with God, and how we can get to know the one, true, living God through His Son, Jesus Christ. We will journey through it all in the Bible! God's Word is powerful and alive, and we get to study it! How wonderful will that be?

I'm thrilled beyond measure that He is our God, and that we can know Him and even fall in love with Him. Praise Him for His Word and for His Son and the Holy Spirit.

The Purpose of this Bible Study

This study is for everyone—whether you don't know if you believe, or if you're a new believer and need some guidance on the basics, or if you're a longtime Christian who wants to fall in love with the Gospel again and learn to walk intimately with our God each day.

Together we're going to study who He is, who we are in relation to Him, and why we need Him so desperately.

Each week, I encourage you to try to spend any time with God you can—early, late, noon, whenever—just to study who He is. When we see ourselves in light of who God is, we can't help but fall to our knees in need of Him. That is such a beautiful thing.

Studying and walking with Him is transforming—no matter where you are right now! He continually transforms us through His Word and His Holy Spirit. And He's always surprising us with how He does it!

C.S. Lewis describes this whole process in a way I love:

Imagine yourself as a living house. God comes in to rebuild that house. At first, perhaps, you can understand what He is doing. He is getting the drains right and stopping the leaks in the roof and so on; you knew that those jobs needed doing and so you are not surprised. But presently He starts knocking the house about in a way that hurts abominably and does not seem to make any sense. What on earth is He up to? The explanation is that He is building quite a different house from the one you thought of—throwing out a new wing here, putting on an extra floor there, running up towers, making courtyards. You thought you were being made into a decent little cottage: but He is building a palace. He intends to come and live in it Himself.

—C.S. Lewis, *Mere Christianity*

He wants to do far more in us than we could ever imagine! Are you ready? Here's the plan for how we'll study the Bible over the next 13 weeks:

week 1—The Bible: The Who, What, When, Where, and Why

week 2—God: Eternal and Loving Creator

week 3—Man, Sin, and the Fall

week 4—Jesus: God in the Flesh

week 5—The Perfect Sacrifice: Why We Needed It

week 6—The Gift of Salvation and Repentance

week 7—Leaving Behind the Darkness

week 8—Believing and Following Jesus Now

week 9—The Holy Spirit: Our Gift

week 10—Grace upon Grace: When We Stumble

week 11—The Transforming Power of the Gospel

week 12—Seeking God's Will in our Lives

week 13—Walking in Joy with an Eternity Mindset

week 1:

The Bible

To begin our study, we're covering the Bible—the who, what, when, where, why, and how of it all. It's important to know from where our Christian beliefs originate. Our faith is rooted firmly in the Bible: the holy, unshakeable Word of God.

the who:

The Bible was written thousands of years ago by men who were inspired by God. *Inspired* means that God told them what to write, and they wrote what He said. Just as you and I write differently, each of the men of God who wrote the Bible did so in his own unique writing voice, but the message these authors conveyed came straight from God:

> *...knowing this first of all, that no prophecy of Scripture comes from someone's own interpretation. For no prophecy was ever produced by the will of man, but men spoke from God as they were carried along by the Holy Spirit.* (2 Peter 1:20-21)

The Bible teaches that all Scripture was given or "breathed out" by God. We read in 2 Timothy 3:16-17:

All Scripture is breathed out by God and profitable for teaching, for reproof, for correction, and for training in righteousness, that the man of God may be complete, equipped for every good work.

the what:

The Bible is broken up into two main sections: the Old Testament and the New Testament.

The Old Testament contains 39 books from Genesis to Malachi. This section was written before Jesus came in the flesh. It tells the story of our beginning (Adam and Eve) and the history of Israel and their interaction with God. The underlying theme is a promise of a Messiah who will come in the future to redeem His people from slavery to sin.

The New Testament begins about 400 years after the Old Testament ends. It is comprised of 27 books, beginning in Matthew with the birth of Jesus and ending in Revelation with a prophecy of what is to come. The New Testament tells of Jesus coming in the flesh, describes the fulfillment of the Old Testament promises, and gives Christians a model of faith to live by until Jesus returns.

the when:

The history of the beginning of the Bible dates back to around 1440 B.C. The last book was estimated to have been completed around A.D. 80-90.

the where:

The simple answer is that the Bible was written in Europe, Egypt, and the Middle East.

the why:

The Bible is God's Word, and it's able to show us the way to salvation. Every word is true and comes from God. The Bible contains so many different stories and letters, but its one central theme is redemption in Jesus Christ. Here is what the Bible says about itself:

But as for you, continue in what you have learned and have firmly believed, knowing from whom you learned it and how from childhood you have been acquainted with the sacred writings, which are able to make you wise for salvation through faith in Christ Jesus. All Scripture is breathed out by God and profitable for teaching, for reproof, for correction, and for training in righteousness, that the man of God may be complete, equipped for every good work. (2 Timothy 3:14-17)

Every word points us to Him. He made us to bring Him glory, and the Bible glorifies our God by showing who He is—a merciful, loving, just Redeemer of sinners like us.

The Bible also gives us instructions on how to live in obedience to God. It shows us what we are supposed to do in life: *"Your word is a lamp to my feet and a light to my path."* (Psalm 119:105) And it keeps us from sin:

How can a young man keep his way pure? By guarding it according to your word. With my whole heart I seek you; let me not wander from your commandments! I have stored up your word in my heart, that I might not sin against you. (Psalm 119:9-12)

the how:

The Bible is so much more than words on a page. It's alive. It contains the words of life—words that bring us to faith in Jesus and convict us of our sin. How does it accomplish this, you may ask? We find the answer in Hebrews 4:12:

For the word of God is living and active, sharper than any two-edged sword, piercing to the division of soul and of spirit, of joints and of marrow, and discerning the thoughts and intentions of the heart.

Reading the Bible is unlike reading anything else. It convicts, and it shows you the truth. It imparts wisdom, and God uses it to change your life.

Soaking your mind in Scripture is so important. There is no law about how often or when, but reading and meditating upon God's Word is something that you should definitely strive to do regularly. Like it says in Psalms—storing His Word in our hearts can keep us from sin.

For me, reading the Bible every day keeps it at the forefront of my mind, ready for action. When I pray, the Holy Spirit uses Scriptures I've read to comfort and direct my heart.

I feel a certain gravity or heaviness in my heart when I read the Word of God. It's like I'm in His presence when I read it, and my heart is getting surgery. It can seem painful, but healing at the same time.

When we hear His truth and take it to heart—seeking to live by it—it convicts us and changes us in ways we never before imagined.

The Bible

week 1: study guide

Read:

    ___2 Timothy 3:15-17   ___2 Peter 1:20-21

    ___Psalm 119:105   ___Psalm 119:09

    ___1 Corinthians 2:7-14   ___1 John 2:20

Take-away theme of these verses:

What do you think?

1. What is the Bible?

2. Based on the above verses, who do you think wrote the Bible?

3. How does the Bible help us as believers?

4. How can it help those who want to know more?

5. Do you think the Bible still applies to us today? How or how not?

How does it apply to me?

6. How do you feel when you read the Bible? What emotions do you experience while meditating on God's Word? Do the passages you read ring true in your heart?

7. If you do believe that the Bible is God's Holy Word, do you read what He wrote on a regular basis? How often?

Assignment: Seeking Him

Do you want to know more of God's Word? Do you wish you had more time to study it? If possible, make reading the Bible the first priority of your day. Beg God to show you a way and give you time to study. He will help you!

Start with just two minutes. Read it in the bathroom, if you have to! Start with just a few verses a day, then increase your reading over time. Don't worry about how much studying others do—it's not a race by any means! Just start and try to stay consistent with a little reading each day.

God can make your heart hunger for His Word if you ask Him. Pray for His help. Ask Him to give you the energy you need to get up earlier. He can do it! He is our Heavenly Father, and He loves to give us good things according to His will.

Pray for His guidance over what to read and when. Read over the verses we are studying each week, and if you would like, start in Psalm 1 and worship God, a few verses at a time. Then, try to add two verses of Proverbs (even if it's over lunch time or before bed!) and ask God for wisdom.

Throughout each day, pray for wisdom. Pray that your heart hungers to seek after God. That kind of intense desire is a gift that He gives us—not something we can muster in our own strength. Have faith that He will do it!

As a journaling exercise, write out your prayer to the Lord this week:

God: Loving and Eternal Creator

Last week we talked about the Bible and why we believe it. This week we get to talk about our God, the Creator of the universe.

Does that thrill you, too? Isn't it a gift that we are allowed to study God freely? We are so blessed to have the freedom to just talk about Him and read about Him—no censors, no fear of being caught. Thank you, Lord!

The deity of God is at the heart of everything we believe as Christians. "Deity" simply means that God is the ultimate King of everything—that all things are under His divine control.

It's important to know who He is. Such knowledge shapes every part of what we believe. For instance, if we believed that God created the world, but then left it alone (as some believe), then we would have to assume that He is neither interested or involved in our daily lives—we would be convinced that everything happens randomly, because God left the world to itself. Instead, it is a comfort to know that He is over all things, because nothing happens outside of His control—every detail is under His care. Isn't that awesome?

So who is God?

He is the Creator of all things.

The very first chapter of the Bible tells us of the world being created by the very words of God. He simply spoke and brought everything—the heavens, earth, water, light, night, day, animals, plants, and trees—into existence. He brought all of the world into being in six days. He formed man *in His own image*, which means that He made man to be a reasoning, emotional being with a will unlike any other creature on the earth. We know God is our creator, and that He made man in his own likeness, because the Bible tells us here in Genesis:

> *Then God said, "Let us make man in our image, after our likeness. And let them have dominion over the fish of the sea and over the birds of the heavens and over the livestock and over all the earth and over every creeping thing that creeps on the earth." So God created man in his own image, in the image of God he created him; male and female he created them. And God blessed them. And God said to them, "Be fruitful and multiply and fill the earth and subdue it and have dominion over the fish of the sea and over the birds of the heavens and over every living thing that moves on the earth."* (Genesis 1:26-28)

He is the Ruler of all things.

God knows everything and is present over all His creation at all times—it's what we call omniscience and omnipresence. He is over all things. I love the way the Psalmist says it best: *"The LORD has established his throne in the heavens, and his kingdom rules over all."* (Psalm 103:19)

There is one God who rules the universe. His kingdom rules over all, and His throne is in the heavens.

Later in 1 Corinthians 8, it tells us again of the story of creation—there is one God, our Father, from whom are all things. He brought everything into existence—and knows everything. And because He created us, it is for Him and His purpose that we exist:

> *... yet for us there is one God, the Father, from whom are all things and for whom we exist, and one Lord, Jesus Christ, through whom are all things and through whom we exist.* (1 Corinthians 8:6)

He is the Father.

In the verse above, God is called Father. He is referred to as "Father" many, many times in the Bible.

This is important to catch. As we looked at Genesis 1, you might have noticed He said "let *Us* make man in *Our* image, after *Our* likeness."

This "Our" is what we call the Trinity. When He says "Our" image, God is referring to Himself, His Son, and His Holy Spirit—one God who exists in three Persons. They are one, together.

This is understandably hard to wrap your mind around. I have believed for more than 25 years, and it's still so much bigger than I can comprehend. God exists in three Persons—each of whom we will talk about in detail individually, but let's say for now that God is the Father, Jesus is the Son, the Holy Spirit is like the divine agent, and they work together with one will.

Keeping what we call the Trinity in mind, we call God the Father because we who are believers are His children. Jesus referred to Him as Father countless times in the New Testament, and He even told us to pray to Him as Father:

> *But when you pray, go into your room and shut the door and pray to your Father who is in secret. And your Father who sees in secret will reward you. And when you pray, do not heap up empty phrases as the Gentiles do, for they think that they will be heard for their many words. Do not be like them, for your Father knows what you need before you ask him. Pray then like this:*

> *"Our Father in heaven, hallowed be your name. Your kingdom come, your will be done, on earth as it is in heaven. Give us this day our daily bread, and forgive us our debts, as we also have forgiven our debtors. And lead us not into temptation, but deliver us from evil."* (Matthew 6:6-13)

The fact that we are His children and He is our Father makes our relationship with God so different from other religions. Did you read that He knows all things before you ask Him? That's the provision of the Father—He cares for us and knows our needs! He is our loving provider of all things.

> *Therefore do not be anxious, saying, "What shall we eat?" or "What shall we drink?" or "What shall we wear?" For the Gentiles seek after all these things, and your heavenly Father knows that you need them all. But seek first the kingdom of God and his righteousness, and all these things will be added to you.* (Matthew 6:31-33)

He is love.

Our Father provides for His children, because He is full of love, goodness, mercy, and grace:

> *The LORD is gracious and merciful, slow to anger and abounding in steadfast love. The LORD is good to all, and his mercy is over all that he has made.* (Psalm 145:8-9)

The Bible is filled with descriptions of God, and the more we study, the more we can learn about His nature. He is *only* good and can do no evil. His mercy is everlasting—which means that it does not run out. He is the epitome of love. The Bible tells us this plainly:

> *Beloved, let us love one another, for love is from God, and whoever loves has been born of God and knows God. Anyone who does not love does not*

know God, because God is love. In this the love of God was made manifest among us, that God sent his only Son into the world, so that we might live through him. In this is love, not that we have loved God but that he loved us and sent his Son to be the propitiation for our sins. (1 John 4:7-10)

His ultimate love was shown through (or made manifest by) God's sending His Son to die for our sins.

He loves us so dearly, so very dearly, that He gave up His Son to be crucified on a cross that we might live instead of die apart from Him!

Oh, isn't that breathtaking?

He is eternal.

God has always been and will always be. This is another incredible thing that humans cannot fully understand. Eternity is a hard thing for us to grasp, but my favorite imperfect illustration that gives you an idea is this:

Imagine stretching a string across an entire football field. Go to the center of it and find one tiny atom, and that's the span of our life in view of eternity. God has existed for more than the entire football field before and after our little atom. He has existed longer, even, than a hundred or a million or a trillion football fields laid end to end in comparison to our tiny little speck on that string.

Lord, you have been our dwelling place in all generations. Before the mountains were brought forth, or ever you had formed the earth and the world, from everlasting to everlasting you are God. You return man to dust and say, "Return, O children of man!" For a thousand years in your sight are but as yesterday when it is past, or as a watch in the night. (Psalm 90:1-4)

Not only is God eternal, but His goodness is eternal, as well. It has always been and will always be: *"For the LORD is good; his steadfast love endures forever, and his faithfulness to all generations."* (Psalm 100:5)

23

God, the Creator of the universe, loves and cares for you—His love endures forever, and His provision for us far exceeds what we can even imagine. God LOVES you. He loves YOU!

That's the best news we could ever hear! We don't deserve His wonderful love, yet He gives it to us anyway! Thank you, Lord, for Your love. We bless Your name, oh Creator, and Giver of all things.

God: Loving and Eternal Creator

week 2: study guide

Read:

___Genesis 1:1-31   ___Ephesians 3:8-9
___Psalm 145:8-9   ___1 Chronicles 29:11
___1 Corinthians 8:6   ___Ephesians 4:5-6

Take-away theme of these verses:

What do you think?

1. First, how do you think of God primarily? As Father? As Creator? As Redeemer?

2. What do the verses above tell you about God and His nature?

3. Do you view God as a loving Father or as an impartial judge or as something else? Why?

How does it apply to me?

4. How do you see yourself in light of the Eternal God who created the earth?

5. How does knowing who God is change your daily life? Or does it?

6. Do you know the love of the Father personally? Do you feel His comfort and love on a regular basis? If not, why do you think that is the case?

Assignment: Seeking Him

Studying who God is helps us to see not only ourselves and who we are, it also brings us great comfort to know that the God of the universe cares and loves us. Each day as you study about Him, spend a few minutes in prayer simply praising God for who He is. Tell Him what you know about Him—even what you just read about Him—in prayer. Praising Him is a form of worship!

It is so good just to praise Him! He brings joy to our souls when we honor Him and when we see how He created and works in everything. Each day, try to thank God for who He is. Focus your thoughts on Him first as you pray. Worshipping Him can change the way you pray and the attitude of your heart throughout the day!

As a journaling exercise, record what you are praising God for this week:

week 3:

Man, Sin, and the Fall

Now that we have a picture of the awesomeness and glory of God, we can talk about man, and who he is in light of the God of the universe.

Without seeing who we are in light of God, we don't understand our place in creation. We are humans—made to glorify and enjoy God, but from the very beginning, we've desired to walk in our way, apart from God's will.

So let's start from the beginning.

Man is created.

Genesis, the first book of the Bible, gives us the details of how humanity began. In the very first chapter, it tells us that God created man on the sixth day in the Garden of Eden:

Then God said, "Let us make man in our image, after our likeness. And let them have dominion over the fish of the sea and over the birds of the heavens and over the livestock and over all the earth and over every creeping thing that creeps on the earth." So God created man in his own image, in the image of God he created him; male and female he created them. (Genesis 1:26-27)

And in the next chapter, we get more of the story:

> *When no bush of the field was yet in the land and no small plant of the field had yet sprung up—for the LORD God had not caused it to rain on the land, and there was no man to work the ground, and a mist was going up from the land and was watering the whole face of the ground—then the LORD God formed the man of dust from the ground and breathed into his nostrils the breath of life, and the man became a living creature. And the LORD God planted a garden in Eden, in the east, and there he put the man whom he had formed. And out of the ground the LORD God made to spring up every tree that is pleasant to the sight and good for food. The tree of life was in the midst of the garden, and the tree of the knowledge of good and evil.* (Genesis 2:5-9)

So there was no man—just the earth, and then God formed the first man and breathed life into him. He gave him a garden, and plants to eat, and wonderful trees whose fruit he was free to enjoy, including the tree of life. In all the garden, there was but one tree from which he was forbidden to eat: the tree of the knowledge of good and evil.

> *The LORD God took the man and put him in the garden of Eden to work it and keep it. And the LORD God commanded the man, saying, "You may surely eat of every tree of the garden, but of the tree of the knowledge of good and evil you shall not eat, for in the day that you eat of it you shall surely die."* (Genesis 2:15-17)

You see, man was created to live forever. He was allowed to eat from the tree of life, which gave eternal life to man. God made the garden of Eden, and walked in fellowship with man there.

Man sins by disobeying God.

But things change. After Eve is created (later, in chapter 2), Satan, the enemy of God, comes to talk to her in the form of a snake. A snake indwelled by Satan talks to a woman? Why, yes.

We know that Satan in the form of the serpent was very deceptive:

Now the serpent was more crafty than any other beast of the field that the LORD God had made. He said to the woman, "Did God actually say, 'You shall not eat of any tree in the garden'?" And the woman said to the serpent, "We may eat of the fruit of the trees in the garden, but God said, 'You shall not eat of the fruit of the tree that is in the midst of the garden, neither shall you touch it, lest you die.'" But the serpent said to the woman, "You will not surely die. For God knows that when you eat of it your eyes will be opened, and you will be like God, knowing good and evil." (Genesis 3:1-5)

So here's the turning point for all of creation. Satan makes Eve doubt what God said, and Eve believes him. Satan sells disobedience to her by offering her the chance to be in a "higher" state: to become like God, knowing good and evil.

So when the woman saw that the tree was good for food, and that it was a delight to the eyes, and that the tree was to be desired to make one wise, she took of its fruit and ate, and she also gave some to her husband who was with her, and he ate. Then the eyes of both were opened, and they knew that they were naked. And they sewed fig leaves together and made themselves loincloths. (Genesis 3:6-7)

So Eve takes of the fruit because of Satan's deception, but Adam eats the fruit from Eve with a full understanding of what he is doing. Adam was not deceived: *"For Adam was formed first, then Eve; and Adam was not deceived, but the woman was deceived and became a transgressor."* (1 Timothy 2:13-14)

Because they ate of the tree of which they were commanded not to, their eyes were opened to good and evil, and they were ashamed of their nakedness. Adam had broken the one and only rule in all of creation, and in doing so, he changed the course of all mankind.

Because they had disobeyed the very Word of God, God brought the promised curse upon both the man and the woman, and they both were destined to die. Adam and Eve could no longer live eternally, because God removed them from the garden and from the tree of life:

> *Then the LORD God said, "Behold, the man has become like one of us in knowing good and evil. Now, lest he reach out his hand and take also of the tree of life and eat, and live forever—" therefore the LORD God sent him out from the garden of Eden to work the ground from which he was taken. He drove out the man, and at the east of the garden of Eden he placed the cherubim and a flaming sword that turned every way to guard the way to the tree of life.* (Genesis 3:22-24)

Sin entered the world and affects all of mankind.

So Adam disobeyed God's command. That is what we call sin. Sin is a breaking of the law that God has set in place. And this disobedience to God's law is in every person's heart. *"Therefore, just as sin came into the world through one man, and death through sin, and so death spread to all men because all sinned."* (Romans 5:12)

Adam's sin brought the curse of death upon all of humanity. Every man and woman born after him has sinned since the beginning (with the exception of Jesus, which we will talk about later).

Every person sins, and every person is destined to die. We see this in our physical realm here on the earth, and the Bible confirms it: *"For all have sinned and fall short of the glory of God."* (Romans 3:23)

And in Romans 3:10 we read:

...as it is written, "None is righteous, no, not one; no one understands; no one seeks for God. All have turned aside; together they have become worthless; no one does good, not even one."

All people are sinners, and none seek after God. This seems hopeless, and it gets worse—but then it gets better.

Man's sin has doomed him to eternal separation from God.

You may think, "But I'm a good person!" That is why the world (those who do not believe) hates the Word of God. The Bible says that none are good. None are righteous before God. It brings to light the sin inside of every person's heart; it reveals that we are all without good.

God is HOLY. He is the perfect God, and only the sinless can come before Him. If you have sinned (even once), you cannot come before God. And all wrongdoing is sin.

Behold, the LORD's hand is not shortened, that it cannot save, or his ear dull, that it cannot hear; but your iniquities have made a separation between you and your God, and your sins have hidden his face from you so that he does not hear. (Isaiah 59:1-2)

Man has ONE hope.

The sin of man—what we call transgression or the going against of God's law —keeps him apart from God and destines him to death. Here is both the bad news and the good news:

For the wages of sin is death, but the free gift of God is eternal life in Christ Jesus our Lord." (Romans 6:23)

The consequences of sin are death and separation from God forever, but God offers a FREE gift of eternal life when you believe in Him! There isn't only bad news after all! Without God, our hearts are self-seeking and full of sin, but when we believe in Jesus, we are made sinless in Him!

By the sacrifice of Jesus, we are made clean from our sin. We can stand before Him as new, righteous children of God when we have faith in Him.

Man, Sin, and the Fall

week 3: study guide

Read:

    ___Genesis 2:15-25   ___Genesis 3:1-19

    ___Romans 5:12   ___Romans 3:23, 6:23

    ___Psalm 14:1-3   ___Psalm 51:1-9

    ___Ephesians 2:1-3   ___1 John 1:9

Define:

sin:

Take-away theme of these verses:

What do you think?

1. Aside from the definition above, what do you think sin is?

2. How did Adam and Eve sin against God in the garden of Eden?

3. What happened to all of mankind when Adam sinned against God?

How does it apply to me?

4. Can you see disobedience to God's laws in your life? How?

5. Do you think it's possible to stop sinning on your own?

6. How does your sin affect your relationship with God today? Is it affecting your walk with Him right now?

Assignment: Seeking Him

Without God, our hearts are full of sin and self-seeking. Even when we walk with Him and believe in Him, we will struggle against sinfulness in our life. As long as we live in these mortal bodies, we will be at war with these desires to live for ourselves.

As believers, we must put to death the sin in our heart each day, and we can only do it with the help of our God, who has conquered sin and death through the sacrifice of His Son, Jesus.

This week, focus on who God is and who we are in light of Him—sinners desperately in need of a Savior to rescue us. It's so important to confess our sins before Him, and to turn away from them with His help.

Sin separates us from God, and when we harbor it in our hearts, we cannot come before Him and keep a close relationship with Him.

We all have sin, so if you are having trouble identifying what sins are in your heart right now, ask God to show you.

Spend a few minutes in prayer, pouring out your heart to God each day this week, begging Him to show you your sin, and to clean your heart from it. It's such an important step to knowing God, and it will be so very sweet to get closer and closer to Him.

As a journaling exercise, you can write here what sins God showed you (and forgave of you!):

Jesus: God in the Flesh

It seems that almost everyone will generally acknowledge that there is a God, but many diverge on the person of Jesus. Few religions of the world believe Jesus is the Son of God, equal to His Father. Yet it's crucial to know who He truly is. So like we always do, let's start from the beginning.

Jesus is the Son of God.

Over and over throughout the New Testament (from Matthew to Revelation), Jesus refers to God as His Father and Himself as the Son, and He even tells us to refer to Him as that, as we see in John 10:30-38:

> *"I and the Father are one." The Jews picked up stones again to stone him. Jesus answered them, "I have shown you many good works from the Father; for which of them are you going to stone me?"*
>
> *The Jews answered him, "It is not for a good work that we are going to stone you but for blasphemy, because you, being a man, make yourself God."*
>
> *Jesus answered them, "Is it not written in your Law, 'I said, you are gods'? If he called them gods to whom the word of God came—and Scripture cannot be broken—do you say of him whom the Father*

consecrated and sent into the world, 'You are blaspheming,' because I said, 'I am the Son of God'? If I am not doing the works of my Father, then do not believe me; but if I do them, even though you do not believe me, believe the works, that you may know and understand that the Father is in me and I am in the Father."

We see it again here, in Matthew 3:16-17:

And when Jesus was baptized, immediately he went up from the water, and behold, the heavens were opened to him, and he saw the Spirit of God descending like a dove and coming to rest on him; and behold, a voice from heaven said, "This is My beloved Son, with whom I am well pleased."

And here in 1 John 2:23:

No one who denies the Son has the Father. Whoever confesses the Son has the Father also.

Jesus existed before the foundation of the world.

From the very beginning, Jesus existed. We come back to the eternity line—those things that are hard to imagine for our limited minds. But from the very beginning, Jesus was present and created the world with God Himself. He is known as the "Word," the very essence and voice of God. Here in the book of John, it tells us how Jesus has always been:

In the beginning was the Word, and the Word was with God, and the Word was God. He was in the beginning with God. All things were made through him, and without him was not any thing made that was made. In him was life, and the life was the light of men. (John 1:1-4)

Jesus became human and lived on this earth.

Here is Jesus as Word again:

And the Word became flesh and dwelt among us, and we have seen his glory, glory as the only Son from the Father, full of grace and truth. (John 1:14)

By a miracle of God, Jesus was born of a virgin. Her name was Mary— and she had never been with a man:

> *In the sixth month the angel Gabriel was sent from God to a city of Galilee named Nazareth, to a virgin betrothed to a man whose name was Joseph, of the house of David. And the virgin's name was Mary. And he came to her and said, "Greetings, O favored one, the Lord is with you!" But she was greatly troubled at the saying, and tried to discern what sort of greeting this might be.*
> *And the angel said to her, "Do not be afraid, Mary, for you have found favor with God. And behold, you will conceive in your womb and bear a son, and you shall call his name Jesus. He will be great and will be called the Son of the Most High. And the Lord God will give to him the throne of his father David, and he will reign over the house of Jacob forever, and of his kingdom there will be no end."*
> *And Mary said to the angel, "How will this be, since I am a virgin?"*
> *And the angel answered her, "The Holy Spirit will come upon you, and the power of the Most High will overshadow you; therefore the child to be born will be called holy—the Son of God."* (Luke 1:26-35)

Jesus was born to Mary in a manger in Bethlehem, and Mary's husband was Joseph. Jesus lived a boy's life and grew in favor with God and man. We don't have many verses about his first thirty years—we just know that his public ministry began at the age of 30 or so.

This is purely speculation, but I imagine that Jesus was a very normal human as a young man, because when He came to minister to His hometown, they rejected Him. They had known Him for years as the son of the carpenter and had trouble viewing Him as anything more than that.

But they were wrong. The Bible tells us clearly that Jesus was God in the flesh:

> *Have this mind among yourselves, which is yours in Christ Jesus, who, though he was in the form of God, did not count equality with God a thing to be grasped, but emptied himself by taking the form of a servant, being born in the likeness of men.*
>
> *And being found in human form, he humbled himself by becoming obedient to the point of death, even death on a cross.*
>
> *Therefore God has highly exalted him and bestowed on him the name that is above every name, so that at the name of Jesus every knee should bow, in heaven and on earth and under the earth, and every tongue confess that Jesus Christ is Lord, to the glory of God the Father.*
> (Philippians 2:5-11)

But what made Jesus so different from anyone else who ever lived?

Jesus lived without sin.

Jesus was the perfect human. He faced the same temptations we do—but He faced them without sinning! It says here in Hebrews 4:14-16:

> *Since then we have a great high priest who has passed through the heavens, Jesus, the Son of God, let us hold fast our confession. For we do not have a high priest who is unable to sympathize with our weaknesses, but one who in every respect has been tempted as we are, yet without sin. Let us then with confidence draw near to the throne of grace, that we may receive mercy and find grace to help in time of need.*

This is essential. The sinless life and sacrificial death of Jesus paid the debt that we owed to God for our own sin.

Jesus was crucified and rose again in three days.

Jesus is perfect. He is a pure and holy light in this dark and evil world. His light exposes the darkness—it uncovers the evil that people harbor in their hearts. The religious people of His time were pretty and spotless on the outside, but were full of deceit and wickedness on the inside. Jesus called them out because He is God and knew the state of their hearts.

When Jesus brought their evil deeds to light, He left no doubt that God despised their hypocrisy. And so the religious people (called the Pharisees) desperately wanted Jesus dead.

The poor, the broken, the hated, and the diseased of this world sought out the light as their hope—while the religious leaders hated Jesus for calling Himself the Son of God, because He was nothing like they thought the Messiah would be. They thought Jesus would come to the earth to rescue them from the Romans who ruled them. They expected Him to come in with trumpets, defeat everyone, and set up His kingdom.

Instead, they saw the son of a poor carpenter from a despised city who claimed He was the Son of God. He did great works in front of them, and these Pharisees had the nerve to say He was of the devil. Oh, my goodness—right?

So they had Jesus put to death. After calling a secret council meeting, they had Jesus arrested. They did this in the middle of the night, because they knew the people would be outraged if they found out about it.

They had hardened their hearts against the Holy God of the universe, and they put Him through torture and hung Him on a cross to die between two thieves.

He died on the cross, a sinless, innocent person, and was buried in a tomb. Three days later, Jesus rose from the dead and for the next forty days appeared to many people. Death had no power over the Son of God; God raised Him from the dead!

Jesus is the mediator between God and man.

Because Jesus put on flesh and lived on the earth as both God and man, died, and rose again, He became the mediator (the peacemaker) between God and man. Without Jesus, we could never stand before God. God is holy and perfect. Our sinful flesh could not stand before His presence—but because Jesus lived a sinless life and sacrificed Himself in our place, He now stands before God as our mediator.

He is at the right hand of God and intercedes on our behalf—which means He brings us before God as holy like He is:

> *Since then we have a great high priest who has passed through the heavens, Jesus, the Son of God, let us hold fast our confession.* (Hebrews 4:14)

This is phenomenal—we have access to God because Jesus paid our debt and presents us as holy before Him!

This sacrifice is a miracle. Because Jesus became man and suffered like us, He knows our weakness and goes to God on our behalf so that we can stand before the holy and amazing God.

Oh, God, who are You that You care so much about our sinful selves? Thank you, Jesus!

Jesus: God in the Flesh

week 4: study guide

Read:

    ___Matthew 1:18-25   ___Philippians 2:5-8

    ___John 1:1, 1:14   ___1 Peter 1:18-21

    ___John 14:6-11   ___Colossians 2:9

    ___Romans 8:3-5   ___Hebrews 4:14-15

Define:

incarnate:

Take-away theme of these verses:

What do you think?

1. Why does it matter that Jesus was born of a virgin?

2. What is so important about the fact that Jesus had no sin?

3. Jesus and God are equal, yet Jesus humbled himself and became obedient even unto death for us on the cross. What does that say about the nature of Jesus?

How does it apply to me?

4. Why do you need Jesus? Do you fully recognize your need for Him?

5. Does knowing that God lived in the flesh (like you) change how you view your relationship with Him each day?

Assignment: Seeking Him

Jesus came to the earth fully God and fully man. He can fully empathize with our weakness in the flesh, because He lived a human life—yet did so without sin. He did this all for us, so that we might put to death sin in our own lives.

His will was to do the will of the Father, because they are One. This week, spend time simply worshipping Jesus. Praise Him for coming to earth, for living and walking among us, for His sacrifice, for His miracles!

Realizing who we are in light of God makes us fall to our knees in brokenness. When we see ourselves for who we are—sinners—we realize that we need someone to redeem us. And that's exactly what Jesus came to do!

Spend some time dwelling on who Jesus is this week. Examine how Jesus has influenced your life up to this point, and long for Him to increase in your life. Ask Him, and He will do it. He is the greatest gift to all of mankind—praise Him for it!

As a journaling exercise, you also can write here of how Jesus has changed your life:

week 5:

The Perfect Sacrifice: Why We Needed It

God (the Father, His Son Jesus, and the Holy Spirit—together all three equal the Trinity) has existed before the foundation of the world. God created man and gave him free will, but man chose to disobey God's command. At that moment, sin entered the world and separated man from God and caused man to become mortal—to die.

Because God is holy, He cannot be in the presence of evil. When man sinned, he could no longer come into the presence of God—instead, he was destined to live in sin until the day he died. He was under the curse of sin, so to speak. You see, the consequence of sin was (and still is) death. Romans 5:12-14 tells us how sin spread among men:

> *Therefore, just as sin came into the world through one man, and death through sin, and so death spread to all men because all sinned—for sin indeed was in the world before the law was given, but sin is not counted where there is no law. Yet death reigned from Adam to Moses, even over those whose sinning was not like the transgression of Adam, who was a type of the one who was to come.*

But God loved man so much that He made a provision for man to atone or to pay for his sins. Because death was the end to sin, a death had to happen in order for man to become blameless. This is what we call a *sacrifice.*

the sacrifice

In the Old Testament (the part of the Bible written in the time before Jesus came), temporary atonement (payment) for sins was made through animal sacrifice. Spotless animals were given at the altar as a sacrifice for sins. The sinless animals took on the sin of the people presenting the sacrifice.

But the problem with the animal sacrifice is that it didn't change the heart of the sinners. It purified them temporarily before God, but they didn't stop sinning or breaking God's law, because sin had not yet been defeated. And so the same sacrifices had to be made over and over and over.

God had created laws and commanded His people to be holy, so that they would see how far short they fall of the mark and be made aware of their sin. But man couldn't keep the laws of God—he kept disobeying them (lying, stealing, coveting, etc.). God was not in any way surprised by this. He knew that this would be the case with man, and from the very beginning, He had a plan to address the problem. Animal sacrifices merely foreshadowed the ultimate Sacrifice that was to come.

the one man

You see, man needed a sacrifice that was perfect: a human who could keep all the laws of God. Someone blameless and holy in God's sight could take the punishment of all of the sins of the world upon His own shoulders, once and for all. One Man's obedience could redeem sinful man and overcome the death that came through Adam at the beginning of the world:

> *Therefore, as one trespass led to condemnation for all men, so one act of righteousness leads to justification and life for all men. For as by the one man's disobedience the many were made sinners, so by the one man's obedience the many will be made righteous. (Romans 5:18-19)*

50

This one Man's name was Jesus. And God knew before He ever founded the world that Jesus would die for the sins of humanity. That He would die for your sins and mine—that He would pay the ultimate price for our breaking of the law by giving His life in exchange for ours:

> *For he grew up before him like a young plant,*
> *and like a root out of dry ground;*
> *he had no form or majesty that we should look at him,*
> *and no beauty that we should desire Him.*
> *He was despised and rejected by men;*
> *a Man of sorrows, and acquainted with grief;*
> *and as One from whom men hide their faces*
> *he was despised, and we esteemed him not.*
> *Surely he has borne our griefs*
> *and carried our sorrows;*
> *yet we esteemed him stricken,*
> *smitten by God, and afflicted.*
> *But he was pierced for our transgressions;*
> *he was crushed for our iniquities;*
> *upon him was the chastisement that brought us peace,*
> *and with his wounds we are healed.*
> *All we like sheep have gone astray;*
> *we have turned—every one—to his own way;*
> *and the LORD has laid on him*
> *the iniquity of us all.* (Isaiah 53:2-6)

Jesus was without sin, but He took our sins upon Himself and died the worst death imaginable on the cross, so that we could have peace with God. On the cross, He was separated from God and bore the penalty for all our sins alone, so we would not have to be separated from God for eternity!

the reason

But why? Why did He, the God of the universe, send His perfect Son to die a sinner's death? Here's the answer: *"For our sake he made him to be sin who knew no sin, so that in him we might become the righteousness of God."* (2 Corinthians 5:21)

He died, and His blood was poured out, so that the just nature of God would be satisfied. The full payment for all our sins was made by Jesus. God did this so we could be blameless in His sight, just like Jesus!

the love

Jesus paid the ransom for you and me, so that we could be reunited with God! He did it to save us, because He loves us so much:

> *For while we were still weak, at the right time Christ died for the ungodly. For one will scarcely die for a righteous person—though perhaps for a good person one would dare even to die— but God shows his love for us in that while we were still sinners, Christ died for us. Since, therefore, we have now been justified by his blood, much more shall we be saved by him from the wrath of God. For if while we were enemies we were reconciled to God by the death of his Son, much more, now that we are reconciled, shall we be saved by his life. More than that, we also rejoice in God through our Lord Jesus Christ, through whom we have now received reconciliation.* (Romans 5:6-11)

Christ died in our place, but He didn't stay dead. God raised Jesus back to life on the third day, because He had defeated death once and for all! The power of sin had been broken. Death could not keep Him in the grave like it does the rest of humanity!

Why did He do it? Why would God send His beloved Son to die and be raised again? He did it for our sake and for His glory:

He was foreknown before the foundation of the world but was made manifest in the last times for the sake of you who through him are believers in God, who raised him from the dead and gave him glory, so that your faith and hope are in God. (1 Peter 1:20-21)

He gave Jesus glory, so that your faith and hope are in God! This was His plan, to unite us to Him as adopted sons and daughters, to grant us forgiveness of our sins, and to show us love by lavishing His grace upon us:

Blessed be the God and Father of our Lord Jesus Christ, who has blessed us in Christ with every spiritual blessing in the heavenly places, even as he chose us in him before the foundation of the world, that we should be holy and blameless before him. In love he predestined us for adoption as sons through Jesus Christ, according to the purpose of his will, to the praise of his glorious grace, with which he has blessed us in the Beloved. In him we have redemption through his blood, the forgiveness of our trespasses, according to the riches of his grace, which he lavished upon us, in all wisdom and insight making known to us the mystery of his will, according to his purpose, which he set forth in Christ as a plan for the fullness of time, to unite all things in him, things in heaven and things on earth. (Ephesians 1:3-10)

God chose us before the foundation of the world to be His children! Isn't that marvelous?

He lovingly offers us this opportunity to come to Him and accept this perfect sacrifice as a free and wonderful gift from Him.

The Perfect Sacrifice: Why We Needed It

week 5: study guide

Read:

    ___John 3:16-17   ___Ephesians 1:1-10

    ___Titus 3:4-6   ___Romans 5:1-21

    ___Hebrews 9:11-28

Define:

covenant:

sacrifice:

Take-away theme of these verses:

What do you think?

1. What did the old, first covenant (before Jesus came) require as a sacrifice?

2. What (or who) was the sacrifice under the new covenant?

3. What is required for the forgiveness of sins (hint: Heb. 9:22)?

How does it apply to me?

4. Do you believe in the sacrifice—that Jesus died for you?

5. How does knowing Jesus died as a sacrifice for your sins change the way you live each day? Or does it?

Assignment: Seeking Him

The sacrifice Jesus made for the sins of the world replaced the old way of doing things through the sacrifice of animals. The sacrifice of His life paid the price for your sins, personally and forever.

Without His blood being poured out—without His death—we cannot approach the throne of God, and we are sentenced to life apart from God for eternity. Sin came into the world through one man, Adam, and the power of sin and death was destroyed by one man on the cross—Jesus.

His sacrifice gives us new life—his resurrection from the dead showed that He defeated and conquered death.

If you believe in Jesus and His sacrifice, and you accept the free gift of salvation, your life will be changed. The free gift of Jesus paying your debt brings you to repentance, for we know that while we were still sinners, Christ died for us. We cannot do anything to be better or to fix ourselves. We are broken and in need of the gift of restoration with God. That is exactly what Jesus' sacrifice offers us: full forgiveness and restored fellowship with Him.

This week, examine your heart in prayer. Are you living with the daily knowledge that Christ died for your sins? Are you walking daily in His grace and strength, or are you doing your own thing and trusting in your own good works to save you? Ask God to show you any areas that need to change.

Pray each day that your heart would seek fully after God. As a journaling exercise, write here how the sacrifice of Jesus has impacted your life today:

The Gift of Salvation and Repentance

We've been hinting at it over and over since we first began this study, but the sacrifice we talked about last week becomes very personal this week. The sacrifice Jesus made by dying on the cross for the sins of mankind—for you and for me—that sacrifice was a gift from God, and it's called salvation. You may accept this gift or reject it. The choice is yours.

What is salvation?

Salvation is being rescued from our sins and their eternal consequences by the One who paid the price for us. A sacrifice had to be made for you to become pure in God's sight—and it's a sacrifice you could neither make on your own nor earn in any way. This is what we call being *justified*. You are made pure—*just*—because Jesus, the Holy Son of God, paid your debt.

What are we "saved" *from*?

When you believe that Jesus is the Son of God and that He died and rose again, defeating death for your sake, you are spared from a life without God here on earth and an eternity spent apart from God in a place called Hell. This is why we call it being saved or receiving the gift of salvation.

We have life on this earth, but the Bible also says we will live eternally—each and every one of us. Those who accept God's gift of salvation will spend eternity with Him in Heaven. Those who reject His offer of forgiveness for sins will spend eternity away from God in Hell.

Every single person on the earth will be judged according to the decision they make concerning Christ, whether to love and trust and accept Him, or to reject Him and refuse the grace and forgiveness of sin He offers:

> *And just as it is appointed for man to die once, and after that comes judgment, so Christ, having been offered once to bear the sins of many, will appear a second time, not to deal with sin but to save those who are eagerly waiting for him.* (Hebrews 9:27-28)

> *When the Son of Man comes in his glory, and all the angels with him, then he will sit on his glorious throne. Before him will be gathered all the nations, and he will separate people one from another as a shepherd separates the sheep from the goats. And he will place the sheep on his right, but the goats on the left.* (Matthew 25:31-33)

Everyone will rise from the dead in the end: For those who believe, they will receive eternal life with Jesus. For those who do not, they receive eternal condemnation apart from God:

> *Do not marvel at this, for an hour is coming when all who are in the tombs will hear his voice and come out, those who have done good to the resurrection of life, and those who have done evil to the resurrection of judgment.* (John 5:28-29)

> *And many of those who sleep in the dust of the earth shall awake, some to everlasting life, and some to shame and everlasting contempt.* (Daniel 12:2)

When the Son of Man comes in his glory, and all the angels with him, then he will sit on his glorious throne. Before him will be gathered all the nations, and he will separate people one from another as a shepherd separates the sheep from the goats. And he will place the sheep on his right, but the goats on the left. Then the King will say to those on his right, "Come, you who are blessed by my Father, inherit the kingdom prepared for you from the foundation of the world." (Matthew 25:31-34)

Then he will say to those on his left, "Depart from me, you cursed, into the eternal fire prepared for the devil and his angels."
(Matthew 25:41)

What does eternal condemnation really look like?

The Bible tells us Hell is a literal place of fiery punishment prepared for those who sin against God to go after they die.

1. It's a place of judgment for those who have sinned.

John, the apostle of Jesus, explains more about what happens to the guilty in the book of Revelation:

Then I saw a great white throne and him who was seated on it. From his presence earth and sky fled away, and no place was found for them. And I saw the dead, great and small, standing before the throne, and books were opened. Then another book was opened, which is the book of life. And the dead were judged by what was written in the books, according to what they had done. And the sea gave up the dead who were in it, Death and Hades gave up the dead who were in them, and they were judged, each one of them, according to what they had done. Then Death and Hades were thrown into the lake of fire. This is the second death, the lake of fire. And if anyone's name was not found written in the book of life, he was thrown into the lake of fire. (Revelation 20:11-15)

61

2. It's full of great sorrow.

The Son of Man will send his angels, and they will gather out of his kingdom all causes of sin and all law-breakers, and throw them into the fiery furnace. In that place there will be weeping and gnashing of teeth. Then the righteous will shine like the sun in the kingdom of their Father. He who has ears, let him hear. (Matthew 13:41-43)

3. It's full of pain and fire.

The Bible describes God's wrath or anger as being poured out like fire:

Who can stand before his indignation? Who can endure the heat of his anger? His wrath is poured out like fire, and the rocks are broken into pieces by him. The LORD is good, a stronghold in the day of trouble; He knows those who take refuge in him. But with an overflowing flood he will make a complete end of the adversaries, and will pursue his enemies into darkness. (Nahum 1:6-8)

And if your right hand causes you to sin, cut it off and throw it away. For it is better that you lose one of your members than that your whole body go into hell. (Matthew 5:30)

Then he will say to those on his left, "Depart from me, you cursed, into the eternal fire prepared for the devil and his angels." (Matthew 25:41)

And if your hand causes you to sin, cut it off. It is better for you to enter life crippled than with two hands to go to hell, to the unquenchable fire. And if your foot causes you to sin, cut it off. It is better for you to enter life lame than with two feet to be thrown into hell. And if your eye causes you to sin, tear it out. It is better for you to enter the kingdom of God with one eye than with two eyes to be thrown into hell, "where their worm does not die and the fire is not quenched." (Mark 9:43-48)

But here's the thing—not only does believing in Jesus save you from eternity in Hell, it saves you from a life lived in sin apart from God right now:

For the wrath of God is revealed from heaven against all ungodliness and unrighteousness of men, who by their unrighteousness suppress the truth. For what can be known about God is plain to them, because God has shown it to them. For his invisible attributes, namely, his eternal power and divine nature, have been clearly perceived, ever since the creation of the world, in the things that have been made. So they are without excuse. (Romans 1:18-20)

And since they did not see fit to acknowledge God, God gave them up to a debased mind to do what ought not to be done. They were filled with all manner of unrighteousness, evil, covetousness, malice. They are full of envy, murder, strife, deceit, maliciousness. They are gossips, slanderers, haters of God, insolent, haughty, boastful, inventors of evil, disobedient to parents, foolish, faithless, heartless, ruthless. Though they know God's righteous decree that those who practice such things deserve to die, they not only do them but give approval to those who practice them. (Romans 1:28-32)

So when you reject God after seeing His creation and hearing His truth, God gives you up to the consequences of your sin—and sin overtakes your life even more.

Believing that Jesus paid the debt you could not, and putting your faith in Him saves you from the consequences of your sins—a life lived in sin and, after death, eternity in Hell away from God. Salvation comes from believing in your heart and confessing with your mouth that Jesus is the Lord:

Because, if you confess with your mouth that Jesus is Lord and believe in your heart that God raised him from the dead, you will be saved. For with the heart one believes and is justified, and with the mouth one confesses and is saved. For the Scripture says, "Everyone who believes in him will not be put to shame." For there is no distinction between Jew and Greek; for the same Lord is Lord of all, bestowing his riches on all who call on him. For "everyone who calls on the name of the Lord will be saved." (Romans 10:9-13)

Believing that Jesus bore your sins on the cross is not just a one-time decision or a single prayer you say. It's a belief that changes the very course of your life—both now and in eternity.

And "everyone who believes will not be put to shame"—if you call on the name of the Lord, you will be saved. Inside your heart you believe, and with your words you outwardly confess that Jesus is Lord—you tell God and others that you believe. You don't have to *do* anything but believe.

If it sounds serious, it is. It really is the biggest decision you can ever make—because it changes your life forever. Those who follow Jesus cannot look the same as the rest of the world. Your heart cannot search for the things the world desires anymore. Your hope is in Jesus! Your joy comes from Him!

Salvation is a free gift that you can accept or reject. It's a wonderful, unbelievably awesome gift, and it's for your good. Believing in the sacrifice of Jesus through the love of God brings repentance to your heart, and the life-transformation that follows is an extraordinarily beautiful thing.

The Gift of Salvation and Repentance

week 6: study guide

Read:

       ___John 3:16,17   ___Acts 16:31

       ___Romans 10:8-13   ___Romans 3:19-26

       ___John 10:25-26   ___Ephesians 2:1-8

       ___John 14:6   ___2 Chronicles 7:14

Define:

salvation:

repentance:

Take-away theme of these verses:

What do you think?

1. There is only one way to be saved. What does the Bible tell us it is?

2. Why is Jesus the only way we can come before the Father?

3. What do you have to do to be saved?

How does it apply to me?

4. Do you believe that Jesus died and was raised on the third day for your sins?

5. If you believe in Jesus, has that belief brought your heart to repentance?

Assignment: Seeking Him

Like we noted last week, if you believe in Jesus and His sacrifice, and if you accept the free gift of salvation, your life can't help but be changed.

The sacrifice Jesus made for you brings you to repentance when you put your trust in Him. When we believe, we begin to see our own sin for what it is, and we desire to turn away from disobedience to God.

It's so important that we repent and turn away from our sinful ways when we follow Jesus. The bad news is that we can't do it alone. The great news is that Jesus can do it for us! He brings us to repentance, and He gives us the ability through the Holy Spirit to become like Him. He gives us the strength to walk in victory over sin. Thanks to His sacrifice, we are slaves to sin no longer. It holds no more power over us. Even so, this kind of repentance is not a work we can do on our own.

This week, examine your heart—test yourself, as Paul says, to see if you are truly in the faith. Do you believe that Jesus Christ paid the price for your salvation? Has that belief changed your life in any way? Or do you seem the same as you were before you believed or as those who have never come to faith? These are hard questions, but they are so important to ask.

Pray that God would reveal what He wants to in your heart this week. Pray that He will show you your sin and bring you to repentance and cleanse your heart from all unrighteousness. He will not turn you away! Keep seeking Him with all your heart—even if you do not know what you believe yet. He will show you!

As a journaling exercise, write here how Jesus is overcoming sin in your life this week:

Leaving Behind the Darkness

Believing in Jesus changes your heart; seeing your sin for what it is brings repentance to your heart and transforms your life through the power of the Holy Spirit.

When you believe in Jesus, the Holy Spirit comes into your heart and begins to bring change to the way you act. This is one of the ways we see God work today—He brings change from the inside out!

Sometimes it's sudden and sometimes it can be a slow process over time, but when you believe, God surely changes your heart to leave behind the ways of the world.

Jesus is the light of the world. Once you believe in Him, you are walking in the light. You can no longer walk in the darkness, because the light shines in the darkness, and darkness is no more.

But what is *darkness*? What are the ways of the world?

the darkness

We know that darkness is sin, but the Bible specifically describes the ways of the world here:

Besides this you know the time, that the hour has come for you to wake from sleep. For salvation is nearer to us now than when we first believed. The night is far gone; the day is at hand. So then let us cast off the works of darkness and put on the armor of light. Let us walk properly as in the daytime, not in orgies and drunkenness, not in sexual immorality and sensuality, not in quarreling and jealousy. But put on the Lord Jesus Christ, and make no provision for the flesh, to gratify its desires. (Romans 13:11-14)

So the works of darkness are things that we probably already recognize as bad or evil: sexual sins, lust, drunkenness, fighting, and jealousy. It seems likely that even non-believers would recognize most of those things as evil, as well.

We find a similar list in 1 Peter 4:

Since therefore Christ suffered in the flesh, arm yourselves with the same way of thinking, for whoever has suffered in the flesh has ceased from sin, so as to live for the rest of the time in the flesh no longer for human passions but for the will of God. For the time that is past suffices for doing what the Gentiles want to do, living in sensuality, passions, drunkenness, orgies, drinking parties, and lawless idolatry. (1 Peter 4:1-3)

Peter adds lust and idolatry (extreme love or worship of someone or something) to the list specifically, as well as carousing (loud drinking and partying).

If you look at the world, especially the American culture, you'll find drinking and immoral sex are commonplace; but they are activities that are not acceptable or pure in the sight of God. Yet, sadly enough, they are almost completely accepted and normal in today's world.

The Bible commands us not to be drunk with wine and not to have sex outside of marriage:

And do not get drunk with wine, for that is debauchery, but be filled with the Spirit. (Ephesians 5:18)

For this is the will of God, your sanctification: that you abstain from sexual immorality; (1 Thessalonians 4:3)

why we leave behind the darkness

When you walk with Jesus, you are done with the ways of the world—you can't live in them anymore. Thanks be to God!

> *If then you have been raised with Christ, seek the things that are above, where Christ is, seated at the right hand of God. Set your minds on things that are above, not on things that are on earth. For you have died, and your life is hidden with Christ in God. When Christ who is your life appears, then you also will appear with Him in glory.*
>
> *Put to death therefore what is earthly in you: sexual immorality, impurity, passion, evil desire, and covetousness, which is idolatry. On account of these the wrath of God is coming. In these you too once walked, when you were living in them. But now you must put them all away: anger, wrath, malice, slander, and obscene talk from your mouth. Do not lie to one another, seeing that you have put off the old self with its practices and have put on the new self, which is being renewed in knowledge after the image of its creator.* (Colossians 3:1-10)

When you walk in the light, you are done with the darkness. You can't stay in those sins. You have to put them away—even things like lying, anger, speaking badly of another person, and hatred are acts of the darkness. Wow, right?

But why are those things so important to avoid? You are the children of God! You are a new creation—made in the image of your Creator. The Bible tells us those who stay in darkness are not going to have a part of the kingdom of God:

> *But sexual immorality and all impurity or covetousness must not even be named among you, as is proper among saints. Let there be no filthiness*

nor foolish talk nor crude joking, which are out of place, but instead let there be thanksgiving. For you may be sure of this, that everyone who is sexually immoral or impure, or who is covetous (that is, an idolater), has no inheritance in the kingdom of Christ and God. (Ephesians 5:3-5)

At one time, you were walking in sin, but now as a child of God you have no place there. You can't keep hanging out with darkness—you can't stay in partnership with it.

Instead, your belief in the truth will shine light on the darkness and expose it for what it is. This might be the hard part for you—leaving behind parts of life that you know so well. You may lose friends or even family when you turn away from your former ways.

When you leave darkness behind, and the ones with whom you used to walk in it, those still in the darkness might be upset and actually say mean things about you. The Bible tells us this in 1 Peter 4:3-5:

For the time that is past suffices for doing what the Gentiles want to do, living in sensuality, passions, drunkenness, orgies, drinking parties, and lawless idolatry. With respect to this they are surprised when you do not join them in the same flood of debauchery, and they malign you; but they will give account to Him who is ready to judge the living and the dead.

You can't stay in the old way of the world, but you are to continually be moving to the light and growing in Christ through the help of the Holy Spirit, so that you can understand the will of God for your life:

Do not be conformed to this world, but be transformed by the renewal of your mind, that by testing you may discern what is the will of God, what is good and acceptable and perfect. (Romans 12:2)

Next week we will discuss what walking in the light looks like, and what the will of God is for the life of the believer.

Leaving Behind the Darkness

week 7: study guide

Read:

___Romans 13:11-14   ___Ephesians 5:3-20

___Romans 12:2   ___1 Peter 4:3-5

___Colossians 3:5-9

Take-away theme of these verses:

What do you think?

1. Based on these verses, what is the "darkness" we are fighting against?

2. Will those who stay in the darkness inherit the kingdom of Heaven?

3. How can you leave behind the darkness and grow in Christ? (hint: Romans 12:2, Romans 13:13-14)

How does it apply to me?

4. Have you ever walked in darkness? What has the Lord rescued you out of?

5. How has He convicted you of sin or walking in the darkness *recently*? Have you seen Him change your heart about a worldly desire you had?

Assignment: Seeking Him

When we talk about laying our lives down before the Lord, it means we are giving Him full control over our lives. When we make the Lord our first and only master, we give up our own desires for His. Doing so actually brings us more joy than any temporary pleasures could ever provide! Sex, beauty, money, success—everything we once loved no longer has power to reign over us. Our desire is for something far better and more satisfying—the Lord Himself!

Because we are sinners, leaving behind the darkness (the world we know and its self-seeking ways) is difficult, but with the help of the Holy Spirit we are given a new desire to live in the light. This week, ask the Lord to reveal to you how you can leave behind the darkness and walk more in the light with Him.

As a journaling exercise, if possible, record how He has recently given you more desire for Him and less desire for the darkness:

week 8:

Believing and Following Jesus Now

So if we leave behind the darkness and all we know, what do we do next? What is the will of God for a believer? It's to walk in the light.

What does the light look like?

But the fruit of the Spirit is love, joy, peace, patience, kindness, goodness, faithfulness, gentleness, self-control; against such things there is no law. And those who belong to Christ Jesus have crucified the flesh with its passions and desires. (Galatians 5:22-24)

Walking in the Spirit or in the light of the Lord, you can't keep feeding those sinful desires—you must put them to death with the power of the cross. Because Jesus defeated sin, He can defeat and put to death the sin that is in you.

Walking in the light means you have love, joy, peace, patience, kindness, goodness, faithfulness, gentleness, self-control. And instead of malice, bitterness, or hatred, when you walk in the light, you have love for your enemies.

Instead of throwing fits of anger or becoming irritated with your family, you can walk in the light by speaking kindly to them and waiting with patience. When someone says something hurtful to you, you walk in the light by controlling your tongue (self-control) and speaking peace-seeking words to them in reply.

If this sounds really hard (or even impossible), that is because it is! Our flesh—our desire to sin—and the Spirit are at war, and we will never be able to win the battle on our own. Our flesh desires to do what is wrong (to say ugly things or get revenge), but the Spirit tells us the right thing to do. It's like a huge war between what God wants and what sin wants in our lives.

But Jesus, in His kindness, saved us *while we were sinners* and rescued us from the chains of our flesh! He has power over sin and death, and with His help, we have the ability to change!

See, this is where we often make a huge mistake as believers. We want to please God by changing ourselves, but our hearts are deceitful, and our flesh is weak.

When we try to do it on our own, we fail, because we aren't relying on God for the change. We are trying to "fix" ourselves. And it feels like an endless cycle. Sometimes we know we can't change, so we get tired of the battle and feel like giving up altogether. We want to stop fighting. But this is where God's grace and strength can be shown—in our weakness!

why we want to walk in the light

The most important thing to realize is that God is the one doing the work in us. It's not about our following some law of *only do this, don't do that*; it's about seeking to do the will of God and to honor Him with our lives.

Giving up our desires and giving up our will is like offering a spiritual sacrifice to God. It pleases Him when we put it all on the altar before Him:

> *I appeal to you therefore, brothers, by the mercies of God, to present your bodies as a living sacrifice, holy and acceptable to God, which is your spiritual worship.* (Romans 12:1)

When you believe and are saved, you have been chosen by God. You are one of His people. You were given mercy and were called out of darkness and into the light. But there remains a war going on against your soul. Darkness—also known as sin or the passions of the flesh—wants to keep you away from God.

But you are a chosen race, a royal priesthood, a holy nation, a people for his own possession, that you may proclaim the excellencies of him who called you out of darkness into his marvelous light. Once you were not a people, but now you are God's people; once you had not received mercy, but now you have received mercy.

Beloved, I urge you as sojourners and exiles to abstain from the passions of the flesh, which wage war against your soul. Keep your conduct among the Gentiles honorable, so that when they speak against you as evildoers, they may see your good deeds and glorify God on the day of visitation. (1 Peter 2:9-12)

That is why we have to walk in the light—we want to walk with honor so that we bring glory to God! You are His child. Walk with Him in joy, love, peace, patience, goodness, kindness.

"All that is good comes from him." (James 1:17) And He empowers us to do these good things. We can do none of them in our own strength, but only through the strength of God.

I love this passage because it sums up so perfectly how we are supposed to live as believers:

Put on then, as God's chosen ones, holy and beloved, compassionate hearts, kindness, humility, meekness, and patience, bearing with one another and, if one has a complaint against another, forgiving each other; as the Lord has forgiven you, so you also must forgive. And above all these put on love, which binds everything together in perfect harmony. And let the peace of Christ rule in your hearts, to which indeed you were called in one body. And be thankful. Let the word of Christ dwell in you richly, teaching and admonishing one another in all wisdom, singing psalms and hymns and spiritual songs, with thankfulness in your hearts to God. And whatever you do, in word or deed, do everything in the name of the Lord Jesus, giving thanks to God the Father through him. (Colossians 3:12-17)

Be thankful. Be humble. Be patient with each other. Love. Forgive. Be kind. Remember, sweet Jesus did all of these things for you first! Dwell on Christ. Do everything for Him. You can do it with His help.

Does that resonate with your spirit, too? I'm in awe of how God works in our hearts to help us desire good things and how He helps us leave behind our desire for darkness.

Oh, God loves us so much to teach us these things! He saved us from the darkness, and it's so important that we don't go back there. Walk in Him—walk in the Light. We can do all these things and more through Christ who gives us strength. (Philippians 4:13)

Believing and Following Jesus Now

week 8: study guide

Read:

___Colossians 3:1-12   ___1 Corinthians 6:9-20
___Ephesians 5:1-20   ___Philippians 2:14-15
___1 Peter 4:1-3   ___1 Samuel 16:7

Define:

immorality:

idolatry:

Take-away theme of these verses:

What do you think?

1. What are believers called to leave behind from their past lives?

2. Why can't believers live in sexual immorality and anger and drunkenness like the rest of the world? (hint: 1 Corinthians 6:17-20)

3. What should a believing person's life look like? (hint: Colossians 3:12-15)

How does it apply to me?

4. Does your life look like the rest of the world's right now?

5. Have you seen God change you from your old ways? If so, how? If not, why do you think you haven't changed?

Assignment: Seeking Him

As we discussed last week, believing and having faith in Jesus will bring you to repentance—to a turning away from the old sinful ways you once loved.

This will look different for everyone. God does His work in each person's heart individually. As believers, we are called to walk in the light—away from the sinful deeds of the darkness—away from being sexually impure, from being drunk, from stealing or lying, from having anger and hatred for others. One cannot live doing these activities and live for Jesus at the same time, because light and darkness cannot abide together.

Jesus is the light that reveals wickedness for what it is. Pray this week that God would bring to light any evil or sin that you may still be walking in, and ask Him to transform you from your old ways and give you strength to walk in the new way—in His light!

Again, it's different for every person, but God deals with the heart inside of us and shows us where we need to repent and follow Him. He loves us too much to leave us in the darkness.

It's a slow process—lifelong even—but God knows just what you need, and you can trust that He is good and loves you more than you will ever know! Oh, may we be pleasing to Him in our daily lives! Seek Him this week and beg Him to transform you out of the old self and into the new.

As a journaling exercise, you also can write here how Jesus has been overcoming evil and transforming your life this week:

week 9:

The Holy Spirit: Our Gift

As a believer, have you ever felt a nudging that you couldn't quite explain, but you just knew it was God? An unspoken whisper in your heart that told you, "Do this..."? And you knew it wasn't your own thought, because not only was it the right thing to do, it was also something you didn't want to do?

That's what it's like when the Holy Spirit is at work in your heart.

The Holy Spirit:

The Holy Spirit is the third person of the Trinity. He is a Spirit, equal with the Father (God) and the Son (Jesus). He is known as the Comforter, the Counselor, and the Helper. He convicts us of our sin; He brings love, joy, and all the good things (the light we talked about last week) to our hearts.

The Holy Spirit might be the most overlooked of the three today, but He actually has a very prominent place in the New Testament. Jesus spoke of Him often and shared more about what the Spirit would do after His death and resurrection. He gave us good news—He promised that the Holy Spirit would be our Helper and would come after He ascended into Heaven:

Nevertheless, I tell you the truth: it is to your advantage that I go away, for if I do not go away, the Helper will not come to you. But if I go, I will send him to you. (John 16:7)

Jesus told us exactly what the Holy Spirit would do:

But the Helper, the Holy Spirit, whom the Father will send in my name, he will teach you all things and bring to your remembrance all that I have said to you. (John 14:26)

So the Holy Spirit is our teacher—He brings wisdom to our hearts straight from the source—from God's Word. He only teaches truth that comes directly from God:

When the Spirit of truth comes, he will guide you into all the truth, for he will not speak on his own authority, but whatever he hears he will speak, and he will declare to you the things that are to come. (John 16:13)

The Spirit testifies to us the truth that Jesus is God:

But when the Helper comes, whom I will send to you from the Father, the Spirit of truth, who proceeds from the Father, he will bear witness about me. (John 15:26)

But Jesus is very clear that the Holy Spirit is for believers alone. The world can't receive His Spirit of truth:

And I will ask the Father, and he will give you another Helper, to be with you forever, even the Spirit of truth, whom the world cannot receive, because it neither sees him nor knows him. You know him, for he dwells with you and will be in you. (John 14:16-17)

Why did God give us this Spirit?

He gave us the Spirit because we are now His children, and He wants us to remember that we are His, and He is our Father:

> *But when the fullness of time had come, God sent forth his Son, born of woman, born under the law, to redeem those who were under the law, so that we might receive adoption as sons. And because you are sons, God has sent the Spirit of his Son into our hearts, crying, "Abba! Father!"* (Galatians 4:4-6)

In the same way a child cries out to his father, we can cry out to our Father in Heaven. We know who our Father is, because the Holy Spirit reminds us: He "bears witness with our spirit that we are children of God." (Romans 8:16)

When our hearts are heavy, when we feel lonely, and when we hurt or disobey—we have a Father in Heaven who loves us and comforts us with His Holy Spirit here on earth. So we know that believers have the Holy Spirit inside of them—that God Himself resides in the hearts of those who've put their faith and trust in Him.

Remember how we talked about animal sacrifices as payment for sins? Before Jesus came, God's presence would only reside in the holy temple. The law and the cleansing of sin by animal sacrifices were required to come before God, but these things were just a shadow of what was to come.

After Jesus died on the cross, there was no longer a reason for holding animal sacrifices in the temple, because Jesus Himself was the ultimate sacrifice for all of mankind.

Furthermore, after Christ died and rose again, there was no longer any need for a physical temple, either. Since Jesus redeemed us, the Holy Spirit can reside in the heart of every believer, because we have been made pure through the blood of Christ. We are clean—and the very *Spirit of God* can dwell in us!! We have become the "temple" of God!

> *Do you not know that you are God's temple and that God's Spirit dwells in you? If anyone destroys God's temple, God will destroy him. For God's temple is holy, and you are that temple.* (1 Corinthians 3:16-17)

87

So because we have been made clean and the Holy Spirit resides in us, we now can offer spiritual sacrifices to God—which means we can give up ourselves, lay down our will, and do good for the glory and purpose of God.

> *I appeal to you therefore, brothers, by the mercies of God, to present your bodies as a living sacrifice, holy and acceptable to God, which is your spiritual worship. Do not be conformed to this world, but be transformed by the renewal of your mind, that by testing you may discern what is the will of God, what is good and acceptable and perfect.* (Romans 12:1-2)

Can we do it on our own?

The answer is, we can't. Not without the help of our Father and His gift to us, the Holy Spirit:

> *So then, brothers, we are debtors, not to the flesh, to live according to the flesh. For if you live according to the flesh you will die, but if by the Spirit you put to death the deeds of the body, you will live. For all who are led by the Spirit of God are sons of God. For you did not receive the spirit of slavery to fall back into fear, but you have received the Spirit of adoption as sons, by whom we cry, "Abba! Father!" The Spirit himself bears witness with our spirit that we are children of God, and if children, then heirs—heirs of God and fellow heirs with Christ, provided we suffer with him in order that we may also be glorified with him.* (Romans 8:12-17)

Because we are the children of God, we are to live like the Son of God lived on this earth—we are to put to death sin and the desires of our flesh. Jesus did it perfectly, so that we can now receive His Spirit and do the same.

Because the Spirit lives in us and tells us what to do, we can't stay the same as we were before. It's like the light and the darkness we talked about previously. The Spirit illuminates the darkness, because He is light.

What does the Spirit at work look like in believers?

If you desire to know more about God, it is because the Holy Spirit is tugging on your heart. When you forgive someone—when your heart leaves that burden of hurt and sadness behind—it's because the Holy Spirit is at work inside you.

When you feel tempted to do something you know is wrong, but your heart tells you not to do it and you run the other way instead—that is the Holy Spirit at work in you. And not only does He tell you to run away, but He gives you the strength to do it!

No temptation has overtaken you that is not common to man. God is faithful, and He will not let you be tempted beyond your ability, but with the temptation He will also provide the way of escape, that you may be able to endure it. (1 Corinthians 10:13)

When you feel a whisper in your heart to give something to someone, to help this person, or to pray for that one right now—that's the Holy Spirit doing His work!

When you walk through a really difficult trial, and you feel joy at the end of it—that's the Holy Spirit refining and changing you!

Strange things may start to happen when you listen to the Holy Spirit. He may tell you to randomly email or call people, and later you'll find out that, at that very moment, the person was crying or needed encouragement! That's when you get chill bumps... because God is over all things, and He sees you!

The Holy Spirit is an extraordinary gift to us as believers—we get to be transformed by Him on a daily basis. He is always revealing our sin, teaching us to do what is right, showing us what the Bible means, giving us wisdom to make decisions, orchestrating the events of our day, helping us forgive and be gracious to others, and changing us to be more and more like Jesus.

That's the thing about salvation—God rescues us from the person that we used to be, and transforms us into a new creation! It sounds too good to be true—

but that's exactly what happens.

The life of a believer is definitely not easy, because you must put to death your own fleshly desires. But at the same time, it's easier to do than you'd ever suspect it would be, because you have the Holy Spirit indwelling you and empowering you to do it. Thank you, Jesus, for giving us the Helper!

The Holy Spirit: Our Gift

week 9: study guide

Read:

    ____John 14:15-26   ____John 15:26

    ____Romans 8:9-11   ____Romans 8:11,16, 26-27

    ____1 John 5:6   ____John 6:63

Take-away theme of these verses:

What do you think?

1. Who is the Holy Spirit?

2. Who receives the power of the Holy Spirit?

3. How does the Holy Spirit help those who believe?

How does it apply to me?

4. Do you feel the Holy Spirit at work in your life?

5. Do you rely on the Holy Spirit in your walk each day? Or is He a silent partner of the Trinity in your life?

Assignment: Seeking Him

The Holy Spirit is God's Spirit. He is the third person of the Trinity, and our comfort and helper. He is as much a part of our lives as Jesus and the Father, but sometimes it's easy to overlook Him in Scripture and in our daily life.

The Holy Spirit guides us each day as to how we are to live for God. It's so important that we develop a relationship and a dependence on Him as we walk with Jesus.

This week, I encourage you to pray specifically that the power and the working of the Holy Spirit will become evident in your life if it isn't already.

The Holy Spirit intercedes for us—He knows our every thought and need before we even ask. That's how wonderful He is!

Ask Him to show His holy power in your life—to guide your path, and to open your eyes to His love for you, then thank Him and give Him praise each day for what you see!

As a journaling exercise, you may write here how you have seen the Holy Spirit working this week:

Grace Upon Grace: When We Stumble

Grace is one of the most beautiful ways your heart is drawn to God. When you experience God's grace, you become even more grateful for His love and kindness toward you.

What is grace?

Really, grace is the very heart of what God has done for us. It's the gift of something we don't deserve: forgiveness of our sins and salvation from spending both life and eternity apart from God.

> *For by grace you have been saved through faith. And this is not your own doing; it is the gift of God, not a result of works, so that no one may boast.* (Ephesians 2:8-9)

We are sinners—we all know that in our hearts—but God is willing and able to rescue us from sin. We were once held hostage by it—we couldn't break free no matter how hard we tried, but Jesus released us from that bondage when He died on the cross. What a gift! When we accept that gift by believing in Him, Jesus enables us to walk in victory over sin: *"For sin will have no dominion over you, since you are not under law but under grace."* (Romans 6:14)

sinning as believers

So we know that we're no longer in bondage to sin and that sin has no more dominion over us, but does that mean believers are completely sinless?

Sadly, it does not. Don't you *wish* you could suddenly be as perfect and sinless as Jesus was? *I know I do.*

But our "flesh"—our mortal body—was conceived by sinful parents (tracing all the way back to Adam and Eve), and it desires to do what our new spirit in Christ does not. As long as we live in mortal flesh, we will struggle with sin, but if we're believers and saved by the Lord Jesus, it will not overcome us.

Let me give you a quick example of how the flesh works: if one of your children or siblings colored on your *favorite* tan leather jacket (you know, the nice one you just got for your birthday) with a sharpie—what would you do when you found it?

If you're anything like me, you'd probably be extremely angry. And the anger would probably come out *vocally,* if you know what I mean. Harsh words, yelling... as you can probably imagine, it wouldn't be pretty.

The horrible tension that bubbles up in your chest and comes out in your thoughts and your words—that's your flesh talking. And somewhere, in the back of your mind, you know you're doing wrong. And you hear a whisper, *"Stop yelling! Be kind...."* That's the Spirit working in you!

You see, right now we are in this middle place. We are not at home—we are at battle in a foreign land, so to speak. Our hearts are being made new and pure by the Holy Spirit, but we let our fleshly bodies win because it feels good at the moment (and sometimes we don't even want to!).

the battle: flesh against spirit

This is what Paul is talking about in Romans 7:

> *For we know that the law is spiritual, but I am of the flesh, sold under sin. For I do not understand my own actions. For I do not do what I want, but I do the very thing I hate. Now if I do what I do not want, I agree*

with the law, that it is good. So now it is no longer I who do it, but sin that dwells within me. For I know that nothing good dwells in me, that is, in my flesh. For I have the desire to do what is right, but not the ability to carry it out. For I do not do the good I want, but the evil I do not want is what I keep on doing. Now if I do what I do not want, it is no longer I who do it, but sin that dwells within me.

So I find it to be a law that when I want to do right, evil lies close at hand. For I delight in the law of God, in my inner being, but I see in my members another law waging war against the law of my mind and making me captive to the law of sin that dwells in my members. Wretched man that I am! Who will deliver me from this body of death? Thanks be to God through Jesus Christ our Lord! So then, I myself serve the law of God with my mind, but with my flesh I serve the law of sin. (Romans 7:14-25)

Paul was feeling the very same struggle that we feel every day: We want to do what is right—our mind says to do it—but our flesh continues to battle against it.

Although our mortal, fleshly bodies are tied to sin, our spirit is not. The Holy Spirit lives in us and has freed us from sin by the power of the cross.

We can't overcome sin with our own power—it has to be God's. And if God lives in us, we cannot with a clear conscience keep committing the old sins we used to love, because the Holy Spirit continually changes us!

the good news: the flesh loses

After explaining the bad new about this battle of the flesh, Paul immediately shares the good news about this battle in chapter 8:

There is therefore now no condemnation for those who are in Christ Jesus. For the law of the Spirit of life has set you free in Christ Jesus from the law of sin and death. For God has done what the law, weakened by the flesh, could not do. By sending his own Son in the likeness of sinful flesh and for sin, he condemned sin in the flesh, in order that the righteous requirement of the law might be fulfilled in us, who walk not according to the flesh but according to the Spirit. For those who live according to the flesh set their minds on the things of the flesh, but those who live according to the Spirit set their minds on the things of the Spirit. For to set the mind on the flesh is death, but to set the mind on the Spirit is life and peace. For the mind that is set on the flesh is hostile to God, for it does not submit to God's law; indeed, it cannot. Those who are in the flesh cannot please God.

You, however, are not in the flesh but in the Spirit, if in fact the Spirit of God dwells in you. Anyone who does not have the Spirit of Christ does not belong to him. But if Christ is in you, although the body is dead because of sin, the Spirit is life because of righteousness. If the Spirit of him who raised Jesus from the dead dwells in you, he who raised Christ Jesus from the dead will also give life to your mortal bodies through his Spirit who dwells in you. (Romans 8:1-11)

The Holy Spirit gives us life. If you believe, even though your mortal body will die because of sin, you are given the gift of life when you walk with Him! God condemned sin in the flesh through the death of Jesus on the cross so that you can have life in Him both now and in eternity.

That means when you believe and follow Jesus—when your mind is set on Him and the Spirit lives in you (and your mind cannot be set on Him *without* the Spirit living in you)—He defeats the sin in your flesh!

This is the gift of grace at work in you! You see, God is putting sin to death where it starts—right inside your heart!

grace works at the heart level

You'll find that when you seek God with all your heart, over time He starts putting sin to death in you more and more. The longer you walk with Christ, the more aware of personal sin you will become.

He gently reminds you when you do sin, too. Thankfully, He keeps working on us over time, helping us to see our sin from His perspective! I am grateful that He is so patient with us!

> *The LORD is merciful and gracious, slow to anger and abounding in steadfast love.* (Psalm 103:8)

Over and over, I stumble and sin. And over and over, He reveals my sin to me, forgives me, and reminds me of what He did for me on the cross. I long to please God more than I ever did before. And that desire has nothing to do with me—nothing at all—but everything to do with the transformative work He has done and continues to do in my heart.

I know myself. I know that had Jesus not redeemed me, I would be more and more lost every year—more deeply selfish, more impatient, more bitter.

But God is so, so merciful to give me grace. He brought me back to life, to know who He is, to *feel* His Spirit, to glory in His presence. I don't deserve that—not one bit of it. Now when I sin and He convicts me, I understand even more of what He has done for me and end up seeking more of Him still! This is His strength being perfected in my weakness! (2 Cor. 12:9)

God is good. Oh, He is so, so merciful! Praise Him for His magnificent grace toward us!

Grace Upon Grace: When We Stumble

week 10: study guide

Read:

     ___Hebrews 4:16   ___1 Corinthians 12:8-9

     ___Romans 6:1-23   ___James 4:5-10

     ___1 John 2:1-3   ___Romans 7:21-25

Take-away theme of these verses:

What do you think?

1. Why is it so hard to live like Jesus wants us to live?

2. How can we overcome our desire to do what is wrong?

3. What is the purpose of our weakness and failures? How do our shortcomings show evidence of God's work in our hearts?

How does it apply to me?

4. Do you feel the war raging inside you like Paul describes in Romans? Do you feel your flesh wanting to do one thing and your spirit longing to do another? Give an example if you can.

5. Has the war that has been happening more often lead you to good—to what God wants—or to the sin side of the conflict? Is there someone in your life with whom you can share these things and who can pray with you about them?

Assignment: Seeking Him

Living for Jesus in our mortal bodies will always be a struggle, but we can't win the battle on our own! God gives us both the Holy Spirit and other believers to help us in our war against sin.

Just know that you have been given grace upon grace—that you are not forsaken in these struggles! God is gracious and slow to anger, and He loves you more than you can ever know.

You can run to Him every single day—minute by minute! If you are in need, He is always there! Pray and cry out to Him, and He will help you in your time of need!

As a journaling exercise, you can write here how you faced a battle against the flesh and its desires and how Jesus delivered you this week:

week 11:

The Transforming Power of the Gospel

Together we've spent 10 weeks going through the story of the Gospel: the story of God and man—and why we need God, and what He has done for us. When you read the Word of God and see God for who He is, you start to understand how desperately you need Him, and you begin to feel so very grateful that He loved you so much to save you! Then you see why the word "Gospel" literally means "the good news!"

I hope you are beginning to understand—with both your heart and your mind—what beautiful things the Lord has done for you. Truly knowing the Lord and who He is completely changes the way you think and live.

Here are just a few ways that believing in the sacrifice and resurrection of Jesus and putting your faith in Him transforms your life:

1. The Gospel allows us to respond graciously to others with love.

When you believe in Jesus, the Holy Spirit dwells within you! You leave behind your old ways and become a new person in Christ. This is what we call conversion. You are converted from walking in sin to walking with God:

> *Therefore, if anyone is in Christ, he is a new creation. The old has passed away; behold, the new has come.* (2 Corinthians 5:17)

105

When the Holy Spirit lives in you, He changes your heart so that you want to live for Him instead of living for yourself, and He enables you to respond to others in ways that show them God has given you a new heart:

And I will give you a new heart, and a new spirit I will put within you. And I will remove the heart of stone from your flesh and give you a heart of flesh. (Ezekiel 36:26)

Remember the sharpie situation from last week? Our natural sinful response to being wronged is to react in anger and/or vengeance. But when the Holy Spirit enters your heart, He starts to overcome your natural, fleshly response!

Here's what life in the Spirit starts to look like: you see the sharpie, you feel the anger rising in your chest, but instead of doing what you feel like doing—immediately yelling—you breathe, and you realize you need to pray for God's help because you are so tempted to lose your temper. (That's the Holy Spirit telling you to pray, by the way.)

You pray something like, "Jesus, I need your help. I'm angry right now. So angry. I need you to calm my spirit, and keep me from sinning and saying something really ugly. God, I know that everything has a reason, and I shouldn't care so much about stuff. Please help me, Lord. Overcome my anger. Please help me to be patient, because I don't feel patient right now."

Then suddenly, your blood pressure starts to fall instead of rise, and somehow God gives you the ability to speak to the culprit with calmness and to forgive them for what they've done. And after it's over, *you know it was God*, because you really wanted to be angry! That's how kind God is! He transforms your heart and your life.

The transforming work of the Holy Spirit enables us to love others. The Gospel at work in our heart allows us to let go of vengeance and do good to our enemies.

2. The Gospel allows us to love others through our actions (a.k.a. our "works").

Through His Spirit, you can forgive when you normally would have still felt angry. You can love when you are hurt. You can hold your tongue when you want to spit back ugliness. This is God—doing things in us that we can't understand or do on our own! It's grace at work. It's the power of the Gospel in our lives.

When we believe and follow Jesus, we obey His commands. Over and over and over again, the Bible says that if we love Jesus we will obey Him. Obeying Him doesn't mean simply following a list of do and don'ts; it means letting God transform our life from the inside out. From our heart to our actions.

Obedience means loving our God and our neighbor like ourselves. Obedience means loving God with all our heart and putting down our idols—the things we care more about than Him (pride, money, success, self-image, entertainment, obsessions, etc.).

Obedience means following Jesus and loving the unloved: visiting the sick, caring for the orphans, putting the needs of others before ourselves. It means serving instead of being served. But it's not about marking things off a checklist—because everyone's opportunities to love and serve will be different.

It's about the heart of the matter: seeking God with everything you have and letting go of earthly pride. This is the power of the Gospel at work in our lives.

When your friends, your family, or even just acquaintances see this crazy change happen in your life, they see the power of God at work in your heart. The Gospel allows us to love others as ourselves, from the heart.

That's how you share the Gospel with others: You can't just talk about it; you have to live it out.

3. The Gospel allows us to face trials with hope.

This is one of the most intriguing ways that the Holy Spirit changes our life. When we face a horrible trial—like terrorist attacks or the death of a child or the loss of a husband or the betrayal of a friend—we are able to face it with the power of God.

When any normal person would *lose hope,* a believer *has hope* because of the promises of God and the comfort of the Holy Spirit. It is incredible to witness the peace of God in a person under trial. It's almost unreal. And it's so beautiful to see.

Trials in the life of a believer shouldn't come as a surprise. They will happen. But we have a Comforter and a Healer who works through our pain and brings us even closer to Him. When we face difficult things in this life, we know they are nothing in comparison to the power and knowledge and plan of our God. And we know that Jesus suffered in the flesh, too, when He was on earth— and He won't leave us alone in our suffering.

> *Beloved, do not be surprised at the fiery trial when it comes upon you to test you, as though something strange were happening to you. But rejoice insofar as you share Christ's sufferings, that you may also rejoice and be glad when his glory is revealed.*
> *Therefore let those who suffer according to God's will entrust their souls to a faithful Creator while doing good.* (1 Peter 4:12-13,19)

When we face a trial, we know that all things work together for the good of those who believe. It's not something that always makes sense to us at the time, but the things that happen in our life are part of God's plan. There is nothing beyond His control, my friend. We can trust Him.

> *And we know that for those who love God all things work together for good, for those who are called according to his purpose.* (Romans 8:28)

It can be so hard for us to see the good God is doing in the midst of our trials, but faith that endures under trial provides even stronger evidence to the world that we truly believe in Jesus. Nothing can separate us from the love of Christ (Romans 8:38-39)! Oh, what a God we serve!

Walking with our Savior changes our life forever. When we believe, we can endure trials, we can show the world Christ's love through our actions, and we can become more and more like Jesus. It's sounds too good to be true, but it's not. It's 100% real.

And it's beautiful. Because He is beautiful. Redeeming the lost, healing the hurt, restoring joy to broken hearts—this is grace upon grace upon grace, sweet friends. He heaps it on us. He mercifully changes our wicked hearts to look more and more like His own.

Oh, to know the true and living God who brings life to your heart and newness to your whole way of thinking!

Thank You, Jesus, for transforming broken and sinful hearts into something beautiful for God's glory!

The Transforming Power of the Gospel

week 11: study guide

Read:

    ___Romans 12:2
    ___Romans 6:5-14
    ___2 Peter 1:3-11

    ___Ephesians 4:17-32
    ___2 Corinthians 4:7-18

Take-away theme of these verses:

What do you think?

1. As believers, what do we have to leave behind from our old ways?

2. What does a transformed life look like? (hint: 1 Peter 1)

3. How does a transformed life display Christ to others?

How does it apply to me?

4. Think of the last two years. Do you see your heart being transformed to be more like Christ? If so, list how. If not, why do you think that is? What has your focus been on?

5. Do you think others see your life being transformed in the past year or two? Have you had a conversation with a friend about the work God is doing (or that's not happening) in your heart lately? Is there someone with whom you can talk about this?

Assignment: Seeking Him

Our lives are a walking testament of God's goodness. He changes our hearts from the inside out, and it brings glory to Him when others see it! When we walk in obedience to Him, our hearts change to be more and more like Him through the power of the Holy Spirit.

We can no longer look like we did in the past because He is continually shaping our hearts! Transformation is a beautiful thing—but it's never easy.

Pray for God to transform your life and, if it's His will, that He might give you a person that you can share this transformation with, whether it's a believer or a non-believer.

As a journaling exercise, write here how God has been working on transforming you from your old sinful ways to walking in obedience to Him:

Seeking God's Will in Our Lives

Have you ever wondered what God's will for your life is?

It's such a challenge to walk by faith when it comes to practical, everyday matters. Where should I live? What should I do? Do I choose this way or that way? What is the most important thing for me to do with this life I've been given? These are some of the questions we all must face.

When we walk with God, we know His will and desires for us because He has spoken of it through His Word, the Bible.

Here's just a small list of what we *know* about God's will for us:

1. He wants us to love Him with all of our hearts.

The most important part of walking with God has nothing to do with where you live or what job you take, or how many times you should volunteer, or how many kids you have. Your first priority in your life is to love God with every single part of your being:

> *And He said to him, "You shall love the Lord your God with all your heart and with all your soul and with all your mind. This is the great and first commandment. And a second is like it: You shall love your neighbor as yourself.* (Matthew 22:37-39)

2. He wants us to love people like we love ourselves.

Jesus very specifically says to love other people like we love ourselves—just like the commandment God gave in the Old Testament. We are to treat the needs of others like they were our own needs. We are to bear the burdens of others as if they were our own.

This is something we cannot do alone. It's way too overwhelming to attempt it in our own strength! But when we love God with all our heart, He shows us or brings to mind specific things we can do to help those around us. He does this through the guiding of His Holy Spirit.

I always love to hear specific, real-life stories of the Holy Spirit at work, so here's one example of what it has looked like for me:

I once read a Craigslist ad in which a lady was venting in detail about her ex-husband as she was trying to sell her furniture. Usually I would go on to the next listing, but for whatever reason, my heart started *hurting for her.*

It was really aching—I felt terrible for this lady who had been so obviously hurt by a man. I couldn't forget about her. I felt like God wanted me to email her. The next morning, I sat down and wrote her an email, telling her what I felt God was laying on my spirit—I told her that I believed He wanted me to tell her He loved her.

I felt like a crazy woman sending an email like that to an anonymous address, but I did it. I couldn't *not* do it.

Just *minutes* later, I got an email back. My heart racing, I opened it as quickly as I could. I let out a sigh of relief as the Craigslist lady thanked me for the sweet email, and told me how it made her smile. *Thank you, Jesus.*

Another minute later I received another email from her. She wrote, "It's so funny that you picked that exact moment to email me... I was just in the middle of a crying breakdown... I think I needed to read your email. Thank you."

And then came my own tears.

God knows what He is doing, sweet friend. I felt like the Holy Spirit was heavy on me to pray for and email this woman. He had a reason for me to do it. And at the exact moment it was needed, He wanted me to share His love with someone else. He works in unexpected ways! Listen to Him if you feel His Spirit telling you to do something. He will guide you and show you how to love others.

3. He will provide for all of our needs.

It is so easy to lose sight of loving God and people when we get busy attending to our daily cares, but whenever we hear Him prompting us to do something, we can be certain that He will provide the resources to do it.

We don't have to worry about *anything*—God already knows our needs. We belong to Him, and He faithfully takes care of His own. We can trust in Him! All we have to do is seek after Him.

> *Therefore, do not be anxious, saying, "What shall we eat?" or "What shall we drink?" or "What shall we wear?" For the Gentiles seek after all these things, and your heavenly Father knows that you need them all. But seek first the kingdom of God and his righteousness, and all these things will be added to you.* (Matthew 6:31-33)

4. He will give us the desires of our hearts when we seek Him.

When we put all our hope and trust in God, He not only directs our path and provides for us, but He also grants us the desires of our hearts.

> *Trust in the LORD, and do good; dwell in the land and befriend faithfulness. Delight yourself in the LORD, and he will give you the desires of your heart. Commit your way to the LORD; trust in him, and he will act.* (Psalm 37:3-5)

When we delight in Him, He meets our needs and gives us what our hearts desire. But here's the catch—it doesn't mean that God just gives us whatever thing or circumstance we happen to desire at that moment.

When we seek after God, our heart wants God *more than anything*. Our hearts want God to do what He wants, not what we want for ourselves. We long to please the one true and living God more than anything else.

When we seek the will of God for our lives, and we trust God to do what is best, He changes our hearts to line up with His. He literally gives us the *desires* of our hearts: He places the desires there in the first place, and then He fulfills them! How kind and gracious He is!

> *If you abide in me, and my words abide in you, ask whatever you wish, and it will be done for you.* (John 15:7)

Walking with Jesus is so much better than you can ever imagine! He is so powerful that He can turn our very hearts to love and wish for the very things *He* desires for us—and then grant in abundance all the things we long for!

5. He wants us to walk in joy and thanksgiving with Him.

No matter how our life turns out—when we seek after God, we know that what He gives us is what He desires for us. The God that created the entire universe can be trusted with our circumstances.

He wants you to take joy in what He gives (or sometimes doesn't give) you, and His will is for you to give thanks in all situations:

> *Rejoice always, pray without ceasing, give thanks in all circumstances; for this is the will of God in Christ Jesus for you.* (1 Thessalonians 5:16-18)

It always comes back to having your eyes set on Jesus. When your hope is in God, you know that no circumstances are out of His control. Nothing surprises Him—He is sovereign over all.

Trusting Him fully changes our perspective—it allows us to rejoice and be thankful, even when we don't know why certain things are happening to us. We just know that we can trust in Him, and His purposes, because we know all things work together for the good of those who love God—for those who are called according to His purpose (that means you, if you are a believer).

118

We like to make life complicated, but it's really very simple: Seek God with all your heart. Love Him with everything you have. Trust Him. And pray for His will to be done in your life. No worry, no fear, no anxiety is needed.

Put your faith in God. He will guide your path.

That's His promise.

Seeking God's Will in Our Lives

week 12: study guide

Read:

    ___1 Thessalonians 5:18   ___Proverbs 3:5-6

    ___Romans 12:2   ___James 1:5, 4:3

    ___1 Peter 2:15   ___Psalm 37:4

Take-away theme of these verses:

What do you think?

1. What are we supposed to do in order for God to lead us?

2. What does our motive have to do with it? (hint: James 4:3)

121

3. What are two things that we know for certain are God's will for us based on the verses above?

How does it apply to me?

4. When you seek God's will in your life, do you ask for His will to be done, or for your specific request to happen?

5. Have you seen God leading your path before? What was the situation? Did it happen when you sought Him with all your heart?

Assignment: Seeking Him

Seeking God's will is something we make far more complicated than it has to be. When we have faith in Him, He directs our steps, and we can trust in the way He leads us. He isn't a God of confusion or fear, but of power, love, and peace.

When we seek after our own desires instead of His, our motives are not pure, but when we seek Him with all our heart, He changes our desires to line up with His will.

How have you sought after God in the past two years? Do you see His work in your life, bending your will to His? Or would you say you chased more after your own longings?

Pray that God would reveal His desire for you this week, and that you will long for His will to be done instead of your own.

As a journaling exercise, you can write here of how God has directed your paths over the years.

Walking in Joy with an Eternity Mindset

Our final week together, we're talking about a crucial part of a believer's life: walking in joy with an eternity mindset.

What does that really even mean, you ask?

It means we can walk daily with Him in great peace and with joy while looking forward to what is to come in eternity. Because we know who God is, we remember what Jesus did for us, and how the Holy Spirit helps us, we know that God is GOD.

He is fully capable of taking care of us, and He is more than trustworthy. When we understand who He is, we realize that we cannot do anything outside of His power. Nothing is outside His control. From Him and through Him and to Him are all things!

walking in joy

That's how we can walk in joy: We know that God is fully in control of our lives and that He is working for His glory and our good. Joy comes when we relinquish control. When we live for God, we can be confident that He has a purpose for whatever He brings into our lives. And that knowledge is freeing!

Even better, when we trust God, when we turn the reins over to Him (or recognize that He's had a firm grasp on them all along), and when we stop worrying about what the future will bring, we are set free to focus on the present and to do so with joy!

Rejoice in the Lord always; again I will say, Rejoice. Let your reasonableness be known to everyone. The Lord is at hand; do not be anxious about anything, but in everything by prayer and supplication with thanksgiving let your requests be made known to God. And the peace of God, which surpasses all understanding, will guard your hearts and your minds in Christ Jesus. (Philippians 4:4-7)

What has God put in your path today? How will you accept it? With joy or with anxiety? Every single day is a gift from God. When we live each day as it comes, being careful to keep our eyes and thoughts focused on Jesus, we can move from one day to the next to the next with Him, until we get to the other side of this life. Eternity with God!

If you are a believer, it helps to think of this life as a marathon—one that requires endurance to the end so that you might receive the prize:

Do you not know that in a race all the runners run, but only one receives the prize? So run that you may obtain it. Every athlete exercises self-control in all things. They do it to receive a perishable wreath, but we an imperishable. (1 Corinthians 9:24-25)

Therefore, since we are surrounded by so great a cloud of witnesses, let us also lay aside every weight, and sin which clings so closely, and let us run with endurance the race that is set before us, looking to Jesus, the founder and perfecter of our faith, who for the joy that was set before him endured the cross, despising the shame, and is seated at the right hand of the throne of God. (Hebrews 12:1-2)

Do you feel weary in your race? Do you wonder if God sees what is happening to you?

Why do you say, O Jacob, and speak, O Israel, "My way is hidden from the LORD, and my right is disregarded by my God"? Have you not known? Have you not heard? The LORD is the everlasting God, the Creator of the ends of the earth. He does not faint or grow weary; His understanding is unsearchable. He gives power to the faint, and to him who has no might He increases strength. Even youths shall faint and be weary, and young men shall fall exhausted; but they who wait for the LORD shall renew their strength; they shall mount up with wings like eagles; they shall run and not be weary; they shall walk and not faint.
(Isaiah 40:27-31)

If you are growing weary in your race right now—don't give up! Seek Him—tell God you are weary, that you need His help to continue following Him. Wait for Him to do it. Trust in His Word. He promises to help you—to give you strength when you seek Him.

When you feel tired, cry out to Him, and give thanks to Him for what He has done. He knows what is happening—He knows you. He planned everything long, long ago:

O LORD, you are my God; I will exalt you; I will praise your name, for you have done wonderful things, plans formed of old, faithful and sure.
(Isaiah 25:1)

God can give you strength to face each day with joy in your soul—even the hardest of days. It's not as much a smile on your face as it is a deep heart happiness—it's knowing that God is in control of everything.

We can rejoice in who He is and what He has done for us, in spite of our circumstances and trials. And that deep faith—believing in the promises of God—produces hope, which brings us an inexpressible joy along with the conviction that this life is not the end.

Eternity lies ahead of us.

walking with an eternity mindset

It's so very important that we keep eternity in mind. Whatever our situation, God has called us to live for Him in this life we've been given. He calls us to obey His Word. To follow Him with all of our hearts. To love others like ourselves. To preach the Gospel to the nations. To run the race with endurance.

It isn't as complicated as we'd like to imagine—He wants us to live our lives fully for Him. And through His Holy Spirit, He empowers us to do His will. When we follow Jesus, we do what He says. We die to our old selves and become born again as a new person.

Yet it's never an easy transformation to become more like Jesus. In fact, the longer you walk with Him, the more sin you will see in your own heart, and the more frequently you will find yourself falling to your knees in repentance.

It's a hard road to follow Jesus and become like Him, but it is entirely possible, thanks to what He did on the cross!

If you aren't walking with God, please, please realize that it's the most important thing that you'll ever do. We have no promise or guarantee of how long this life will last. If you've been putting off a relationship with God, you need to keep this fact in mind. There may be no tomorrow for you.

Oh, please hear this: God loves you. If you believe, He redeemed you by spilling the blood of His precious Son. Don't reject Him. Don't harden your heart today. If you don't follow God's Word—if you don't seek after God—chances are, you aren't a follower of God.

If God's Word isn't changing your life, you're not experiencing what you should be. I can't tell you what you are or aren't by any means, but take a deep look within your own heart (2 Cor. 13:5). You know what is true. And if you can't see it, ask God. He will show you.

There are no perfect people, other than Jesus. We all experience ups and downs in our walk with God. But if your spirit is consistently dry, if you rarely pray or read God's Word (even though you may go to church and work in Sunday School), then you are missing out on knowing the one true and living God.

Now is the time to seek Him. Not later.

Don't ignore the stirring in your heart. Go and sit today and pray for God to show you what you need to know. God hears the cries of His people. He sees your heart, your sin, your struggles. He is the one true and living God. He is jealous for your heart—don't let your job, your school, your spouse, your busyness, or even your parenting role get in the way of knowing Him.

You have a call on your life—one to glorify God with everything you do. Don't chase after yourself—chase hard after God. His joy is so much better than we could ever imagine. And we have yet to even talk about what will happen in eternity!

When we seek after Him—when we give our lives to Him in faith, believing that His Word is true, that His Son has defeated death and sin, and that we have the Holy Spirit—our lives are changed. The outcome of our faith is a royal inheritance: our salvation and life in eternity with God in Heaven:

Blessed be the God and Father of our Lord Jesus Christ! According to his great mercy, he has caused us to be born again to a living hope through the resurrection of Jesus Christ from the dead, to an inheritance that is imperishable, undefiled, and unfading, kept in heaven for you, who by God's power are being guarded through faith for a salvation ready to be revealed in the last time. In this you rejoice, though now for a little while, if necessary, you have been grieved by various trials, so that the tested genuineness of your faith—more precious than gold that perishes though it is tested by fire—may be found to result in praise and glory and honor at the revelation of Jesus Christ. Though you have not seen him, you love him. Though you do not now see him, you believe in him and rejoice with joy that is inexpressible and filled with glory, obtaining the outcome of your faith, the salvation of your souls. (1 Peter 1:3-9)

Your faith will be tested. Will it stand? Will it result in praise and glory and honor when Jesus returns? Do you love Him even though you haven't seen Him? Do you rejoice in who God is? Do you know Him? Does He know you?

The Lord is able to change your life. He is able to see you to your final day—to complete the work that He began in you:

And I am sure of this, that he who began a good work in you will bring it to completion at the day of Jesus Christ. (Philippians 1:6)

If there is one thing you take away from this study, I hope it will be this: You have one chance to live for God on this earth. Love Him with all your heart—seek after Him with everything you have. Even if it means losing everything that you know. He is more than worth it. Seek Him as if your life depends on it, because it does. All life depends on Him.

If you are already walking with Him, I encourage you to take Jude's words to heart:

But you, beloved, building yourselves up in your most holy faith and praying in the Holy Spirit, keep yourselves in the love of God, waiting for the mercy of our Lord Jesus Christ that leads to eternal life. (Jude 1:20-21)

Jesus will return for His people. He is coming back, though none of us know when. My prayer is that we will be faithful until the end. Don't let sin overtake your life and cause you to live apart from God. You can't be a follower of God if you don't follow God.

Take care, brothers, lest there be in any of you an evil, unbelieving heart, leading you to fall away from the living God. But exhort one another every day, as long as it is called "today," that none of you may be hardened by the deceitfulness of sin. For we have come to share in Christ, if indeed we hold our original confidence firm to the end. (Hebrews 3:12-14)

Those warnings keep us awake, keep us seeking God, don't they? They don't give us cause to fear—they remind us of what our purpose is here on earth.

We can believe with great confidence that God is able to keep us from sin and able to present us blameless at the end through Jesus. He chose us before the foundation of the world! He set us apart to be adopted in Christ as part of His will! He has even promised to give us a guarantee of our inheritance, the Holy Spirit:

> *Blessed be the God and Father of our Lord Jesus Christ, who has blessed us in Christ with every spiritual blessing in the heavenly places, even as he chose us in him before the foundation of the world, that we should be holy and blameless before him. In love he predestined us for adoption as sons through Jesus Christ, according to the purpose of His will, to the praise of his glorious grace, with which he has blessed us in the Beloved. In him we have redemption through his blood, the forgiveness of our trespasses, according to the riches of his grace, which he lavished upon us, in all wisdom and insight making known to us the mystery of his will, according to his purpose, which he set forth in Christ as a plan for the fullness of time, to unite all things in him, things in heaven and things on earth.*
>
> *In him we have obtained an inheritance, having been predestined according to the purpose of him who works all things according to the counsel of his will, so that we who were the first to hope in Christ might be to the praise of his glory. In him you also, when you heard the word of truth, the gospel of your salvation, and believed in him, were sealed with the promised Holy Spirit, who is the guarantee of our inheritance until we acquire possession of it, to the praise of his glory. (Ephesians 1:3-14)*

This is the very essence of the Gospel: God redeeming the broken—changing lives. Taking sinners and making them His children, forgiving their sins and freely giving them salvation and life with Him for eternity through His Son! How could we possibly not want to give all of ourselves to Him?

Walking in Joy with an Eternity Mindset

week 13: study guide

Read:

___Romans 8:28

___Hebrews 12:1

___John 15:1-11

___Colossians 3:17

___Philippians 1:6

___Romans 2:6-11

___John 16:24

Take-away theme of these verses:

What do you think?

1. How do we continue to walk (abide) in God's love?

2. What promise of completion does the believer have in Christ? (also see Jeremiah 29:11)

3. Why is it important that we are steadfast in our walk with Him—that we stay in the race to the end?

How does it apply to me?

4. Do you feel like you are walking intimately with God right now? Are you moving forward in Christ?

5. What are ways you can continue to grow in Christ in your life? Are there daily activities that you could do for Him and His glory instead of your own? (maybe through a perspective change?)

Assignment: Seeking Him

God wants you to abide in Him throughout your time here on earth. He can keep you safe and help you to finish the race of this life. Ask in His name that He would see your life to completion in Him, and then trust that He will do it!

We can walk with Him every single day, every single hour, every single minute. In everything we do, God wants us to live in His name—walking with joy and giving Him the glory.

If you want to walk with Him like this, just ask Him. Ask in the name of Jesus that He will transform your life—that everything you do will be for His purpose and His glory. He won't deny you! He is so good! And even better, God will give you joy through your journey with Him.

As we close this study, think about the ways God has transformed your life in recent years. Remember the things He has done for you, and thank Him for them. Ask Him to continue to do His work in you.

Oh, Jesus, we praise you for redeeming our souls. You are the merciful, sovereign God. Please keep us safe from the evil one and help us to endure until the end.

As a journaling exercise, you can write here of what God has done in your life recently—how He has kept you safe or taught you more about Him.

Conclusion

Together we've spent 13 weeks studying the good news of Jesus! Can you believe we're here already? Do you feel like you know more about the Gospel than when we first began? But more than just gathering new facts, do you truly believe that Jesus, the Son of God, died and rose again from the dead for *you*?

When you believe this good news of the Gospel is true, your life will be forever changed. And when you put your faith in Jesus, your very heart will change too! You'll be able to repent from your sin and be given a new heart, new desires, and a new hope. You will understand the Gospel in the deepest parts of your soul, because the eyes of your heart will be opened to the truth of who you are, and what Jesus did for *you*.

Then suddenly, without any effort on your part, you will *know* the lovely taste of that Gala apple we first talked about, because you will have *experienced* it yourself. The beautiful Gospel of Jesus Christ redeeming you is the one thing you'll be able to savor for the rest of your life; both here and in eternity.

If you ask me, there's nothing sweeter in the entire world.

Oh, taste and see that the LORD is good! Blessed is the man who takes refuge in him! (Psalm 34:8)

Acknowledgements

I am so grateful to my husband Robert, for his love for me and his steady encouragement to put this project together. Without your support, babe, I would have never been able to finish. Your passion for preaching the Gospel continuously moves me to do hard things and go outside of my comfort zone. I love you so.

I'm also entirely and happily indebted to Jennifer and Doug Flanders for the existence of this project in the book format. Your skills and knowledge are without a doubt the only reason anyone is reading this book. I am blessed beyond measure to know you, and words cannot express how grateful I am for your help and your countless hours of editing. Only the Lord could orchestrate such a miracle as the sweet gift you have given to me. Thank you.

And to my parents: Thank you for loving me and first pointing me to the Lord, and for the years you spent investing in my heart and mind. I love you.

About the Author

Mandy Ballard is a woman born again
only by the grace of God,
the wife of a sweet man named Robert,
and a homeschooling mama of seven.
She desires to glorify God
in her everyday life
and considers homemaking a radical, hard,
and wonderful calling of the Lord.
You can find Mandy writing each week
about life at home, parenting, faith and more
at http://www.biblicalhomemaking.com.

Connect with Mandy through social media

 https://www.facebook.com/biblicalhomemaking

https://twitter.com/bhomemaking

https://www.instagram.com/bhomemaking/

https://www.pinterest.com/bhomemaking/

more Christian Living titles from

Prescott Publishing

25 Ways to Communicate Respect to Your Husband:
A Handbook for Wives

Jennifer Flanders

25 Ways to Show Love to Your Wife:
A Handbook for Husbands

Doug Flanders, MD

Balance:
The Art of Minding What Matters Most

Jennifer Flanders

Life's Big Questions:
A Study Guide for the Book of Colossians

Doug Flanders

Love Your Husband/ Love Yourself:
Embracing God's Purpose for Passion in Marriage

Jennifer Flanders

visit Mandy's blog:

Biblical Homemaking

Mandy writes: *"My desire for Biblical Homemaking is that it would be an encouragement to other women who are in the same place as I am—serving God in everyday homemaking. May our time be well spent in serving Him—whether it be in homemaking, parenting, marriage, creating, baking, cleaning, or just living life!*

www.biblicalhomemaking.com

Made in the USA
Columbia, SC
03 November 2017